# Teach Yourself
## Internet and
## World Wide Web,
### Second Edition

⟨ **W9-AMT-208**

IDG's **3-D Visual** Series

**IDG BOOKS**   *From* **maranGraphics**™

IDG Books Worldwide, Inc.
An International Data Group Company
Foster City, CA  •  Indianapolis  •  Chicago  •  New York

## Teach Yourself Internet and World Wide Web VISUALLY,™ 2nd Ed.

Published by
**IDG Books Worldwide, Inc.**
An International Data Group Company
919 E. Hillsdale Blvd., Suite 400
Foster City, CA 94404

Copyright© 1999 by maranGraphics Inc.
5755 Coopers Avenue
Mississauga, Ontario, Canada
L4Z 1R9

Library of Congress Catalog Card No.: 99-066847
ISBN: 0-7645-3410-6
Printed in the United States of America
10 9 8 7 6 5 4 3 2 1

Distributed in the United States by IDG Books Worldwide, Inc.
Distributed by CDG Books Canada Inc. for Canada; by Transworld Publishers Limited in the United Kingdom; by IDG Norge Books for Norway; by IDG Sweden Books for Sweden; by Woodslane Pty. Ltd. for Australia; by Woodslane (NZ) Ltd. for New Zealand; by TransQuest Publishers Pte Ltd. for Singapore, Malaysia, Thailand, Indonesia, and Hong Kong; by ICG Muse, Inc. for Japan; by Norma Comunicaciones S.A. for Colombia; by Intersoft for South Africa; by Le Monde en Tique for France; by International Thomson Publishing for Germany, Austria and Switzerland; by Distribuidora Cuspide for Argentina; by Livraria Cultura for Brazil; by Ediciones ZETA S.C.R. Ltda. for Peru; by WS Computer Publishing Corporation, Inc., for the Philippines; by Contemporanea de Ediciones for Venezuela; by Express Computer Distributors for the Caribbean and West Indies; by Micronesia Media Distributor, Inc. for Micronesia; by Grupo Editorial Norma S.A. for Guatemala; by Chips Computadoras S.A. de C.V. for Mexico; by Editorial Norma de Panama S.A. for Panama; by American Bookshops for Finland. Authorized Sales Agent: Anthony Rudkin Associates for the Middle East and North Africa.
For corporate orders, please call maranGraphics at 800-469-6616.
For general information on IDG Books Worldwide's books in the U.S., please call our Consumer Customer Service department at 800-762-2974.
For reseller information, including discounts and premium sales, please call our Reseller Customer Service department at 800-434-3422.
For information on where to purchase IDG Books Worldwide's books outside the U.S., please contact our International Sales department at 317-596-5530 or fax 317-596-5692.
For consumer information on foreign language translations, please contact our Customer Service department at 1-800-434-3422, fax 317-596-5692, or e-mail rights@idgbooks.com.
For information on licensing foreign or domestic rights, please phone 1-650-655-3109.
For sales inquiries and special prices for bulk quantities, please contact our Sales department at 650-655-3200.
For information on using IDG Books Worldwide's books in the classroom or for ordering examination copies, please contact our Educational Sales department at 800-434-2086 or fax 317-596-5499.
For press review copies, author interviews, or other publicity information, please contact our Public Relations department at 650-655-3000 or fax 650-655-3299.
For authorization to photocopy items for corporate, personal, or educational use, please contact maranGraphics at 800-469-6616.
Screen shots displayed in this book are based on pre-release software and are subject to change.

## Trademark Acknowledgments

**©1999 maranGraphics, Inc.**

The 3-D illustrations are the
copyright of maranGraphics, Inc.

| **U.S. Corporate Sales** | **U.S. Trade Sales** |
| --- | --- |
| Contact maranGraphics at (800) 469-6616 or Fax (905) 890-9434. | Contact IDG Books at (800) 434-3422 or (650) 655-3000. |

# ABOUT IDG BOOKS WORLDWIDE

Welcome to the world of IDG Books Worldwide.

IDG Books Worldwide, Inc., is a subsidiary of International Data Group, the world's largest publisher of computer-related information and the leading global provider of information services on information technology. IDG was founded more than 30 years ago by Patrick J. McGovern and now employs more than 9,000 people worldwide. IDG publishes more than 290 computer publications in over 75 countries. More than 90 million people read one or more IDG publications each month.

Launched in 1990, IDG Books Worldwide is today the #1 publisher of best-selling computer books in the United States. We are proud to have received eight awards from the Computer Press Association in recognition of editorial excellence and three from Computer Currents' First Annual Readers' Choice Awards. Our best-selling *...For Dummies®* series has more than 50 million copies in print with translations in 31 languages. IDG Books Worldwide, through a joint venture with IDG's Hi-Tech Beijing, became the first U.S. publisher to publish a computer book in the People's Republic of China. In record time, IDG Books Worldwide has become the first choice for millions of readers around the world who want to learn how to better manage their businesses.

Our mission is simple: Every one of our books is designed to bring extra value and skill-building instructions to the reader. Our books are written by experts who understand and care about our readers. The knowledge base of our editorial staff comes from years of experience in publishing, education, and journalism — experience we use to produce books to carry us into the new millennium. In short, we care about books, so we attract the best people. We devote special attention to details such as audience, interior design, use of icons, and illustrations. And because we use an efficient process of authoring, editing, and desktop publishing our books electronically, we can spend more time ensuring superior content and less time on the technicalities of making books.

You can count on our commitment to deliver high-quality books at competitive prices on topics you want to read about. At IDG Books Worldwide, we continue in the IDG tradition of delivering quality for more than 30 years. You'll find no better book on a subject than one from IDG Books Worldwide.

John Kilcullen
Chairman and CEO
IDG Books Worldwide, Inc.

Steven Berkowitz
President and Publisher
IDG Books Worldwide, Inc.

**VIII**
WINNER

*Eighth Annual
Computer Press
Awards ≥ 1992*

**IX**
WINNER

*Ninth Annual
Computer Press
Awards ≥ 1993*

*1994 COMPUTER CURRENTS READERS CHOICE*

**X**
WINNER

*Tenth Annual
Computer Press
Awards ≥ 1994*

**XI**
WINNER

*Eleventh Annual
Computer Press
Awards ≥ 1995*

IDG is the world's leading IT media, research and exposition company. Founded in 1964, IDG had 1997 revenues of $2.05 billion and has more than 9,000 employees worldwide. IDG offers the widest range of media options that reach IT buyers in 75 countries representing 95% of worldwide IT spending. IDG's diverse product and services portfolio spans six key areas including print publishing, online publishing, expositions and conferences, market research, education and training, and global marketing services. More than 90 million people read one or more of IDG's 290 magazines and newspapers, including IDG's leading global brands — Computerworld, PC World, Network World, Macworld and the Channel World family of publications. IDG Books Worldwide is one of the fastest-growing computer book publishers in the world, with more than 700 titles in 36 languages. The "...For Dummies®" series alone has more than 50 million copies in print. IDG offers online users the largest network of technology-specific Web sites around the world through IDG.net (http://www.idg.net), which comprises more than 225 targeted Web sites in 55 countries worldwide. International Data Corporation (IDC) is the world's largest provider of information technology data, analysis and consulting, with research centers in over 41 countries and more than 400 research analysts worldwide. IDG World Expo is a leading producer of more than 168 globally branded conferences and expositions in 35 countries including E3 (Electronic Entertainment Expo), Macworld Expo, ComNet, Windows World Expo, ICE (Internet Commerce Expo), Agenda, DEMO, and Spotlight. IDG's training subsidiary, ExecuTrain, is the world's largest computer training company, with more than 230 locations worldwide and 785 training courses. IDG Marketing Services helps industry-leading IT companies build international brand recognition by developing global integrated marketing programs via IDG's print, online and exposition products worldwide. Further information about the company can be found at www.idg.com.
1/24/99

maranGraphics is a family-run business
located near Toronto, Canada.

At **maranGraphics**, we believe
in producing great computer
books–one book at a time.

Each maranGraphics book
uses the award-winning
communication process that
we have been developing over
the last 25 years. Using this
process, we organize screen
shots, text and illustrations in
a way that makes it easy for
you to learn new concepts
and tasks.

We spend hours deciding
the best way to perform each
task, so you don't have to!
Our clear, easy-to-follow
screen shots and instructions
walk you through each task
from beginning to end.

Our detailed illustrations go
hand-in-hand with the text to
help reinforce the information.
Each illustration is a labor of
love–some take up to a week
to draw!

We want to thank you for
purchasing what we feel
are the best computer
books money can buy.
We hope you enjoy using
this book as much as we
enjoyed creating it!

Sincerely,

*The Maran Family*

Please visit us on the web at:
# www.maran.com

## CREDITS

**Authors:**
Kelleigh Wing
Paul Whitehead
Ruth Maran

**Copy Editor:**
Roxanne Van Damme

**Project Manager:**
Judy Maran

**Editing &
Screen Captures:**
Raquel Scott
Janice Boyer
Michelle Kirchner
James Menzies
Stacey Morrison

**Layout & Illustrations:**
Treena Lees

**Illustrators:**
Russ Marini
Jamie Bell
Peter Grecco
Sean Johannesen
Steven Schaerer

**Screens & Illustrations:**
Jimmy Tam

**Permissions Coordinator:**
Jenn Hillman

**Indexer:**
Raquel Scott

**Post Production:**
Robert Maran

**Editorial Support:**
Barry Pruett
Martine Edwards

## ACKNOWLEDGMENTS

Thanks to the dedicated staff of maranGraphics, including
Jamie Bell, Cathy Benn, Janice Boyer, Peter Grecco,
Jenn Hillman, Sean Johannesen, Michelle Kirchner,
Wanda Lawrie, Frances Lea, Treena Lees, Jill Maran, Judy Maran,
Robert Maran, Sherry Maran, Russ Marini, James Menzies,
Stacey Morrison, Steven Schaerer, Raquel Scott, Jimmy Tam,
Roxanne Van Damme, Paul Whitehead and Kelleigh Wing.

Finally, to Richard Maran who originated the easy-to-use
graphic format of this guide. Thank you for your
inspiration and guidance.

# Permissions

## Allaire
Copyright © Allaire Corporation 1995-1999. All rights reserved. Used by permission.

## AltaVista
Digital, AltaVista and the AltaVista logo are trademarks or service marks of Digital Equipment Corporation. Used with permission.

## Apple Computer
Macintosh is a trademark of Apple Computer Inc., registered in the United States and other countries. Screen shots reprinted with permission from Apple Computer, Inc.

## Ask Jeeves
Ask Jeeves is a trademark of Ask Jeeves, Inc., Copyright 1996-1999 Ask Jeeves, Inc.

## CareerMosaic
CareerMosaic 1999. All rights reserved.

## CNET
Reprinted with permission from CNET, Inc. © 1995-9. CNET.com

## CouponSurfer.com
Copyright © 1998-1999 CouponSurfer.com, Inc. All rights reserved.

## CyberPatrol
© 1998 The Learning Company, Inc.

## Deja.com
Courtesy of Deja.com.™

## Dell
Dell computer used with permission from Dell Corporation.

## Excite
Copyright © 1995-99 Excite, Inc. All rights reserved.

## Exploratorium
Reproduced by permission. Copyright 1999 Exploratorium, www.exploratorium.com

## Go.com
Reprinted by permission. Infoseek, Ultraseek, Ultraseek Server, Quickseek, the Infoseek logos and the tagline "Once you know, you know" are trademarks of Infoseek Corporation which may be registered in certain jurisdictions. Other trademarks shown are trademarks of their respective owners. Copyright © 1994-1998 Infoseek Corporation. All rights reserved. GO Network is a trademark of Disney Enterprises, Inc., 1998-1999, Infoseek Corporation authorized licensee.

## Greek Mythology
Copyright 1993-1998. Mythweb, Fleet Gazelle.

## Happy Puppy
©1999 Attitude Network, Ltd., part of theglobe.com Network. All rights reserved. Happy Puppy and Happy Puppy Logo are service marks of Attitude Network, Ltd.

## Institute for Molecular Virology
© 1994-1999 Stephan Spencer, Jean-Yves Sgro, and the Internet Concepts LLC.

## Internet Movie Database
Copyright © 1990-1999. The Internet Movie Database.

## Ipswitch
Copyright 1991-1999, Ipswitch, Inc.

## Jazz Online
Copyright 1991-1999 Jazz Online. ® All rights reserved.

## Kabuki for Everyone
Copyright Kabuki for Everyone.

## Kids' Space
Copyright 1995-1997 Kids' Space.™ All rights reserved.

## Lighthouses
Copyright 1995-1998 David S. Carter, Donald W. Carter & Diana K. Carter. All rights reserved.

## Lotus
© 1999 Lotus Development Corporation. Used with permission of Lotus Development Corporation. Lotus is a registered trademark of Lotus Development Corporation.

## Microsoft Corporation
Screen shots reprinted with permission from Microsoft Corporation.
Box shot reprinted with permission from Microsoft Corporation.

## National Climatic Data Center
Source: National Oceanic and Atmospheric Administration, National Climatic Data Center, Asheville, North Carolina.

## Netscape
Portions Copyright Netscape Communications Corporation, 1999. All Rights reserved. Netscape, Netscape Navigator and the Netscape N Logo, are registered trademarks of Netscape in the United States and other countries.

# TABLE OF CONTENTS

## Chapter 1

### The Internet

## Chapter 2

### Connect to the Internet

## Chapter 3

### The World Wide Web

# Chapter 4

**Web Page Enhancements**

# Chapter 5

**Search the Web**

# TABLE OF CONTENTS

## Chapter 6

### Create Web Pages

## Chapter 7

### Download Information from the Internet

## Chapter 8

### Electronic Mail

# Chapter 9

**Mailing Lists**

# Chapter 10

**Newsgroups**

# Chapter 11

**Chat**

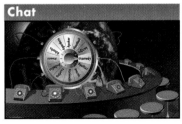

# TABLE OF CONTENTS

## Chapter 12

### Multi-Player Games

## Chapter 13

### Intranets

## Chapter 14

### Interesting Web Sites

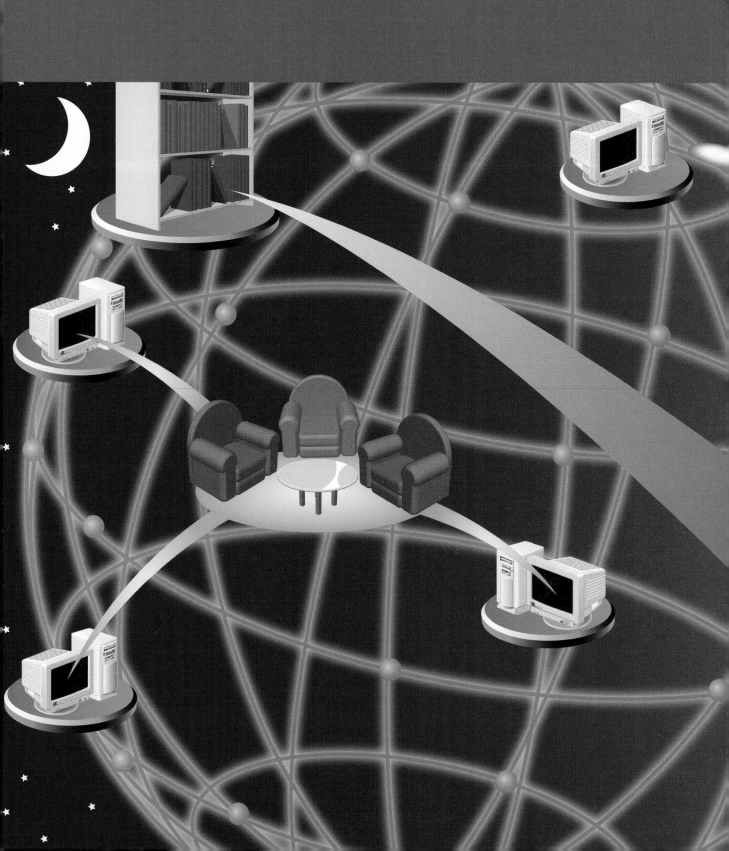

## CHAPTER 1

# The Internet

*Are you curious about the Internet?
This chapter explains what the
Internet is and how it works.*

# INTRODUCTION TO THE INTERNET

**The Internet is the largest computer network in the world.**

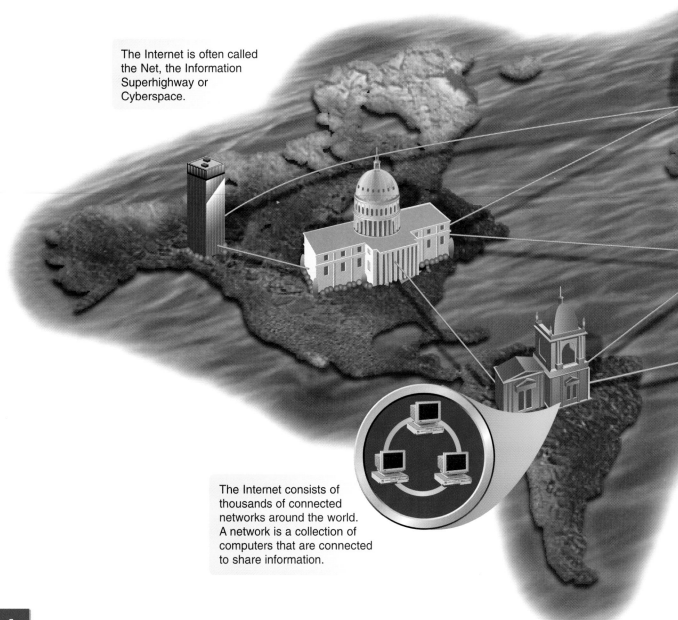

The Internet is often called the Net, the Information Superhighway or Cyberspace.

The Internet consists of thousands of connected networks around the world. A network is a collection of computers that are connected to share information.

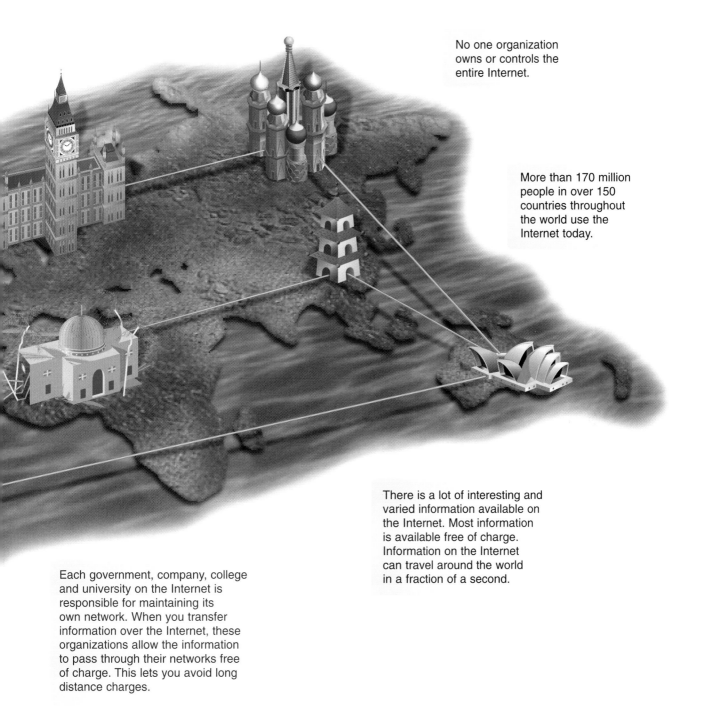

No one organization owns or controls the entire Internet.

More than 170 million people in over 150 countries throughout the world use the Internet today.

There is a lot of interesting and varied information available on the Internet. Most information is available free of charge. Information on the Internet can travel around the world in a fraction of a second.

Each government, company, college and university on the Internet is responsible for maintaining its own network. When you transfer information over the Internet, these organizations allow the information to pass through their networks free of charge. This lets you avoid long distance charges.

# WHAT THE INTERNET OFFERS

## ELECTRONIC MAIL

Electronic mail (e-mail) is the most popular feature on the Internet. You can exchange electronic mail with people around the world, including friends, family members, colleagues, customers and even people you meet on the Internet. Electronic mail is fast, easy, inexpensive and saves paper.

## INFORMATION

The Internet gives you access to information on any subject imaginable. This makes the Internet a valuable research tool. You can review newspapers, magazines, academic papers, government documents, famous speeches, job listings, airline schedules and much more.

## ENTERTAINMENT

The Internet offers many different forms of entertainment, such as radio and television broadcasts, videos and music. You can find pictures from the latest films, watch live interviews with your favorite celebrities and listen to music before it is available in stores. You can also play interactive games with other people around the world.

## DISCUSSION GROUPS

You can join discussion groups on the Internet to meet people around the world with similar interests. You can ask questions, discuss problems and read interesting stories. There are thousands of discussion groups on topics such as the environment, food, humor, sports and television.

## CHAT

The chat feature allows you to exchange typed messages with another person on the Internet. A message you send will instantly appear on the other person's computer.

## PROGRAMS

You can find programs to use on your computer, such as word processors and games. You can also obtain programs, called shareware, that you can try for free for a limited time. If you like the program and want to continue using it, you must pay the author of the program.

## ONLINE SHOPPING

You can order products on the Internet without leaving your desk. You can purchase items such as books, flowers, music CDs, pizza, stocks and used cars.

# WHO USES THE INTERNET

**People of all ages and backgrounds use the Internet.**

## CHILDREN

The Internet can help children improve their reading and communication skills. Children can send e-mail messages to their friends and explore information on the Internet. Many security products are available that allow children to access the Internet without being exposed to inappropriate material.

## PEOPLE AT HOME

There are many services and resources available for people who use the Internet at home. People can use the Internet to access information about their community, such as local newspapers, television listings and movie theater showtimes. People can also use the Internet to find restaurant reviews and purchase tickets for sporting events.

## STUDENTS

Many students can access the Internet directly from school. The Internet contains a vast amount of information that can assist students with school projects. Students can also use the Internet to communicate with students in other parts of the world to learn new languages and learn about different cultures. High school students can use the Internet to find information on colleges or universities they are interested in attending.

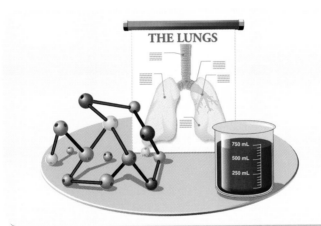

## RESEARCHERS

One of the original uses for the Internet was to help researchers and scientists at universities around the world exchange information and work on joint projects. Information displayed on the Internet allows researchers from different parts of the world to work together.

## PEOPLE AT WORK

Many people use the Internet at work. People can communicate with colleagues and clients using e-mail or videoconferencing over the Internet. People can also use the Internet to perform many business tasks, such as ordering products from other companies, shipping packages around the world and performing banking transactions.

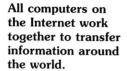

All computers on the Internet work together to transfer information around the world.

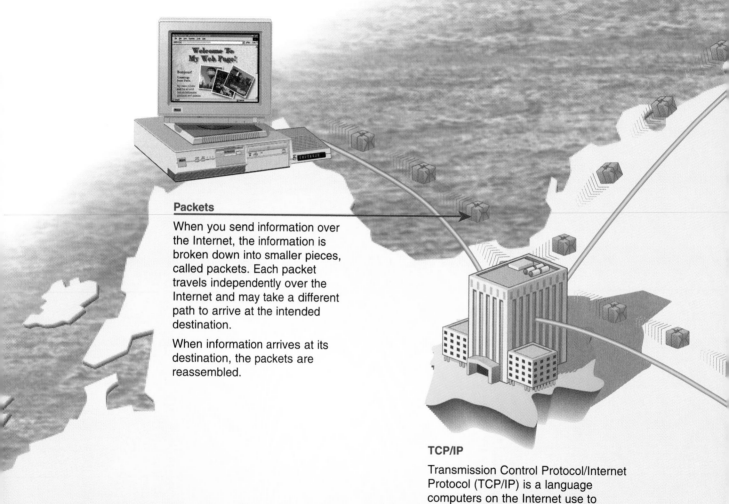

### Packets

When you send information over the Internet, the information is broken down into smaller pieces, called packets. Each packet travels independently over the Internet and may take a different path to arrive at the intended destination.

When information arrives at its destination, the packets are reassembled.

### TCP/IP

Transmission Control Protocol/Internet Protocol (TCP/IP) is a language computers on the Internet use to communicate with each other. TCP/IP divides information you send into packets and sends the packets over the Internet. When information arrives at the intended destination, TCP/IP ensures that all the packets arrived safely.

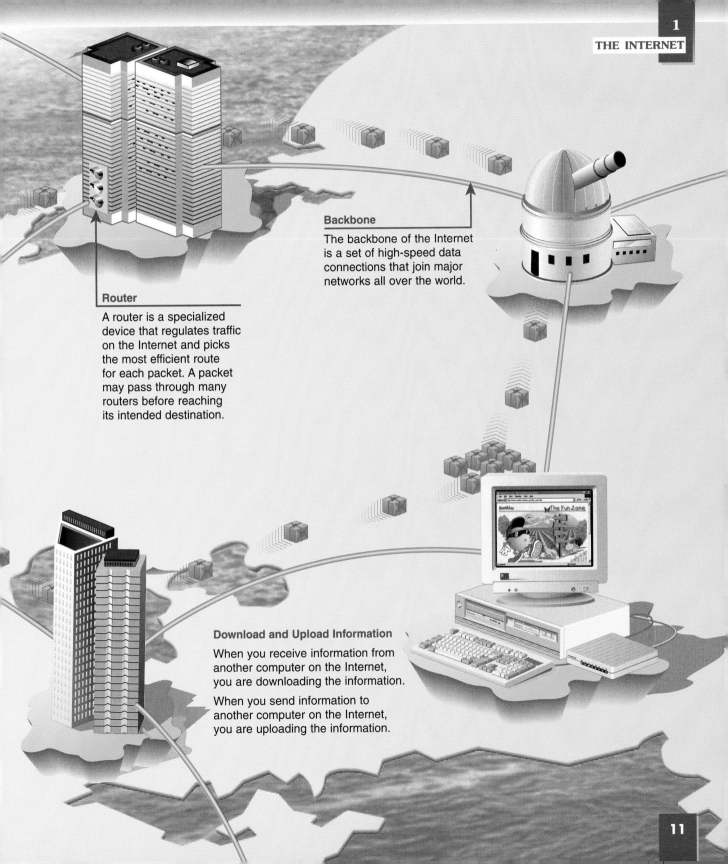

### Backbone

The backbone of the Internet is a set of high-speed data connections that join major networks all over the world.

### Router

A router is a specialized device that regulates traffic on the Internet and picks the most efficient route for each packet. A packet may pass through many routers before reaching its intended destination.

### Download and Upload Information

When you receive information from another computer on the Internet, you are downloading the information.

When you send information to another computer on the Internet, you are uploading the information.

# HOW THE INTERNET STARTED

The Internet was created by combining the ideas and talents of many people. Organizations and individuals have worked together for many years to make the Internet the valuable resource it is today.

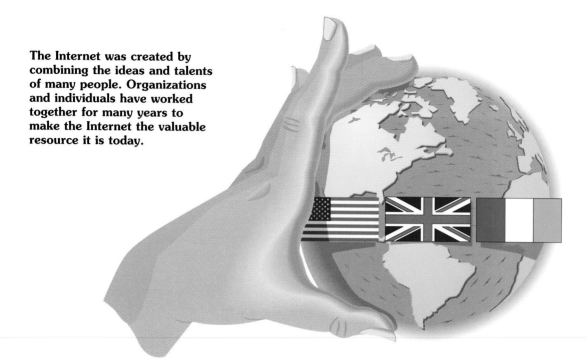

**ARPANET**

In the late 1960s, the U.S. Defense Department created a network that linked military computers together. The network, called ARPANET, was connected in a way that ensured that if one section of the network was damaged, the remaining computers on the network would still be able to communicate with each other.

**NSFNET**

The National Science Foundation created NSFNET in the mid-1980s. NSFNET used the technology developed for ARPANET to allow universities and schools to connect to each other. By 1987, NSFNET could no longer handle the amount of information that was being transferred. The National Science Foundation improved the network to allow more information to transfer. This improved, high-speed network became the Internet.

## PUBLIC ACCESS

In the 1980s, most of the people accessing the Internet were scientists and researchers. In the early 1990s, many companies started to offer access to home users. This allowed anyone with a modem and a computer to access the Internet.

## THE WORLD WIDE WEB

The World Wide Web was created in the early 1990s by the European Laboratory for Particle Physics. The goal of the World Wide Web was to allow researchers to work together on projects and to make project information easily accessible. The first publicly accessible Web site was created in 1991.

## COMPANY WEB SITES

By the mid-1990s, over 30 million people had access to the Internet. To reach this huge market, most big companies created their own sites on the World Wide Web to sell or provide information about their products. There are now thousands of companies on the Web.

## CHAPTER 2

# Connect to the Internet

*Do you want to get connected to the Internet? Find out about the equipment and services that help you connect in this chapter.*

# GETTING CONNECTED

**You need an Internet access provider, equipment and software to connect to the Internet.**

## INTERNET ACCESS PROVIDER

### Internet Service Provider or Commercial Online Service

Internet Service Providers (ISP) and commercial online services are companies that give you access to the Internet for a fee. Make sure you choose an ISP or online service with a local telephone number to avoid long distance charges.

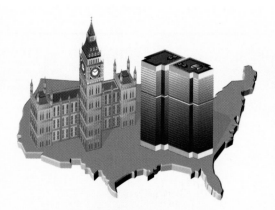

### University, Company or Library

There are many ways you can access the Internet for free. Universities and colleges often provide students and teachers with free access to the Internet. Many companies also provide free Internet access for their employees. Your local library may also offer free Internet access.

## COMPUTER

You can use any type of computer, such as an IBM-compatible or Macintosh computer, to connect to the Internet.

Some operating systems allow you to connect to the Internet through one computer on a network. This is useful if all the computers on the network must share one connection.

## MODEM OR HIGH-SPEED CONNECTION

You need a modem or high-speed connection to connect to the Internet. For more information, see pages 18 to 21.

## SOFTWARE

Most computers come with software to help you set up the computer to access the Internet. For example, computers that come with Windows 98 include the Internet Connection Wizard.

You also need software, such as a Web browser, to access information on the Internet. Most new computers come with this software installed.

## USER NAME AND PASSWORD

You have to enter a user name and password when you want to connect to the Internet. This ensures that you are the only one who can access your Internet account. Your Internet access provider will usually supply you with a user name and password.

# MODEMS

A modem is a device that lets computers communicate through telephone lines. Modems provide an easy way to access information on the Internet.

## TYPES OF MODEMS

An internal modem is a circuit board inside a computer. An external modem is a small box that uses a cable to connect to the back of a computer. Internal modems are less expensive than external modems but are more difficult to set up.

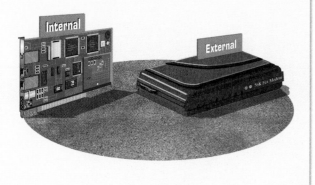

## SPEED

The speed of a modem determines how fast it can send and receive information through telephone lines. Faster modems transfer information more quickly, so they can save you time and may reduce your online service charges. Modem speed is measured in Kilobits per second (Kbps). You should buy a modem with a speed of at least 56 Kbps.

## PHONE LINE

You use the same phone line for telephone and modem calls. When you use a modem to access the Internet, you will not be able to use the phone line for telephone calls. If your telephone and modem share the same line, make sure you turn off the call waiting feature when using your modem, since this feature could disrupt the modem connection.

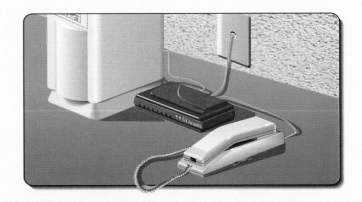

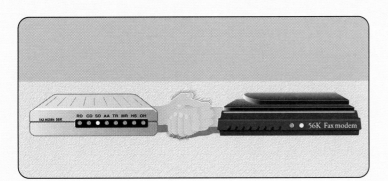

## HANDSHAKE

When your modem first contacts another modem, you may hear a series of squeals and signals. This is called a handshake. Just as two people shake hands to greet each other, modems perform a handshake to establish how they will exchange information.

## ONLINE

You are online when your modem has successfully connected to another modem. This means the modems are ready and able to exchange information. When your modem is not connected to another modem, you are offline.

# HIGH-SPEED CONNECTIONS

**There are several types of high-speed connections you can use to connect to the Internet instead of using a modem.**

Using a high-speed connection does not tie up your telephone line while you are on the Internet, so you can make phone calls while you are connected to the Internet.

## ISDN

An Integrated Services Digital Network (ISDN) line is a digital phone line offered by telephone companies in most cities. An ISDN line can transfer information at speeds from 56 Kbps to 128 Kbps.

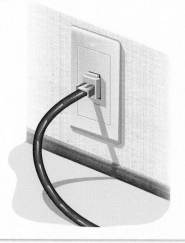

## CABLE MODEM

A cable modem allows you to connect to the Internet with the same type of cable that attaches to a television set. A cable modem can transfer information at a speed up to 3,000 Kbps. You can contact your local cable company to determine if they offer cable Internet service.

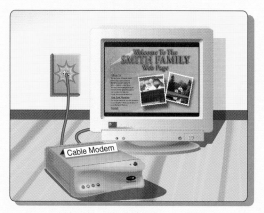

## DSL

Digital Subscriber Line (DSL) is a high-speed digital phone line service offered by telephone companies in many cities. DSL can transfer information at speeds from 1,000 Kbps to 6,000 Kbps.

## DIRECT CONNECTION

A direct connection allows you to connect your computer directly to the Internet. T1 and T3 are the two most popular speeds of direct connection lines. T1 lines can transfer information between the Internet access provider and your home at speeds up to 1,500 Kbps. T3 lines can transfer information at speeds up to 44,000 Kbps.

## FUTURE TECHNOLOGIES

In the future, you may be able to use two-way satellites or even electric power lines to connect and transfer information on the Internet. Companies are constantly working on ways to send more information at faster speeds. With these types of high-speed connections, people will be able to participate in high-quality, live videoconferencing or even watch a movie on the Internet.

# WIRELESS ACCESS

You can use a wireless modem to access information on the Internet without using a phone line or other physical connection.

Wireless access to the Internet allows you to check your e-mail or look up your favorite Web site while you are waiting at the airport, commuting on a train or even stuck in a traffic jam.

## RADIO TECHNOLOGY

Some wireless modems use radio technology to transfer information between computers. A wireless modem communicates with radio transceivers often mounted on streetlights and utility poles. Currently you can only access the Internet using radio technology in certain cities, on some college campuses and at major airports.

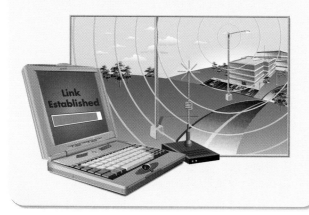

## CELLULAR TECHNOLOGY

Some wireless modems connect to the Internet using the same cellular networks as cellular phones use. Cellular networks exist in most areas so Internet access is more widely available than access using radio technology.

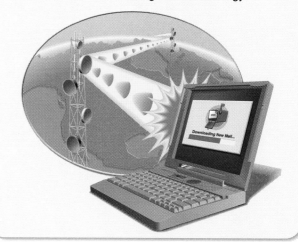

## WIRELESS DEVICES

### CELLULAR PHONES

Some companies are beginning to incorporate Internet features into their cellular phones. For example, you can use a cellular phone to access e-mail messages or find text-based information on the Internet. The phones can also store information such as a calendar, to-do list or contact list.

### HANDHELD COMPUTERS

You can use a handheld computer to exchange e-mail messages and access information on the Internet. Handheld computers are also capable of storing thousands of addresses, appointments and memos. Some handheld computers have a keyboard, while others let you use a stylus, or electronic pen, to input information.

### NOTEBOOK COMPUTERS

Notebook computers often have the same capabilities as a desktop computer and can run the same programs. Notebook computers can use a wireless connection to access information on the Internet, but usually also have a modem that you can use with a standard phone line when wireless access is not available.

# INTERNET SERVICE PROVIDERS

An Internet Service Provider (ISP) is a company that gives you access to the Internet for a fee.

## FIND AN ISP

Ask friends, relatives and colleagues in your area which Internet service provider they use and if they are happy with the service. You can also check the telephone directory to find a list of service providers in your area. Before you choose an ISP, you may want to ask for references from other customers. This can help you find out about the reliability and performance of the ISP.

## ACCESS NUMBERS

Most Internet service providers let you connect to the Internet by dialing a local telephone number. Some service providers also have a toll free number you can use. This allows you to connect to the Internet without long distance charges, even when you are traveling.

## COST

There are different ways an Internet service provider can charge you for the time you spend on the Internet. Many service providers offer a certain number of hours per month for a set fee. If you exceed the total number of hours, you are usually charged for every extra hour.

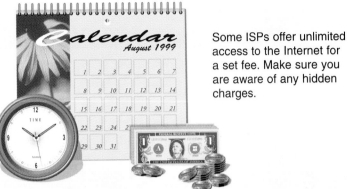

Some ISPs offer unlimited access to the Internet for a set fee. Make sure you are aware of any hidden charges.

## DISCOUNTS

You should find out if the Internet service provider you are considering offers any discounts. Some Internet service providers offer a discount if you pay for an entire year instead of paying each month. Some of the larger service providers even offer a free computer if you sign up for a specific length of time.

## TRIAL PERIOD

Some Internet service providers allow potential customers to use their service free of charge for a limited time. This allows you to fully evaluate the service provider before paying for the service.

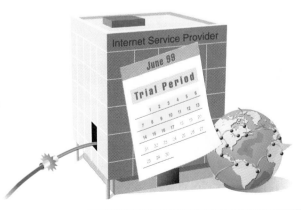

# INTERNET SERVICE PROVIDERS (CONTINUED)

## BUSY SIGNALS

If you use a modem to connect to an Internet service provider, ask the ISP how often users get a busy signal when trying to connect during the most popular connection times, such as evenings and weekends. If you hear a busy signal when you try to connect, you cannot access the Internet at that time.

## CUSTOMER SUPPORT

Setting up a connection to an Internet service provider can be a difficult process. Find out if the ISP offers customer support in the evenings and on weekends as well as during business hours.

## WEB PAGE PUBLISHING

You can create Web pages to share business or personal information with people around the world. Many Internet service providers let you publish and maintain your own Web pages for free. Many service providers also provide software to help you create your Web pages.

## SOFTWARE

Most Internet service providers offer free software that lets you access information on the Internet. This software usually includes a program that lets you exchange e-mail and a program that lets you browse through information on the Web.

## FAMILY SERVICES

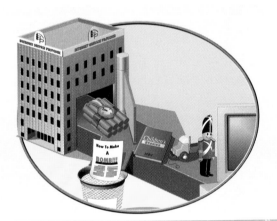

Some ISPs offer a service that can block access to offensive or illegal information on the Internet for you. If you are concerned about the type of information your family has access to on the Internet, you should find out if the service provider can block information.

## MULTIPLE E-MAIL ADDRESSES

Many Internet service providers allow you to have multiple e-mail addresses for one Internet account. This is useful if you want each member of your family to have their own personal e-mail address.

# COMMERCIAL ONLINE SERVICES

**A commercial online service is a company that offers a vast amount of information and access to the Internet for a fee.**

The America Online® Service (AOL) is the most popular commercial online service. The Microsoft Network (MSN) and CompuServe are also popular services.

## WELL-ORGANIZED INFORMATION

Commercial online services provide an enormous amount of well-organized information and services such as daily news, weather reports, encyclopedias and chat rooms.

## EASE OF USE

Using a commercial online service is often the least complicated way of getting connected and using the Internet. Most commercial online services allow you to use one program to access all the features of the service, such as chat rooms, the Internet and e-mail. The program provided by a commercial online service is usually very graphical and easy to use.

## SOFTWARE

Most commercial online services provide software that makes it simple for you to connect to the service. This software is usually very easy to install on a computer. You can also upgrade to the latest version of the software while you are connected to the service.

## INTERNET ACCESS

Commercial online services provide their members with an online community where they can access information and meet new people, but the services also offer access to the whole Internet, including e-mail and information on the World Wide Web.

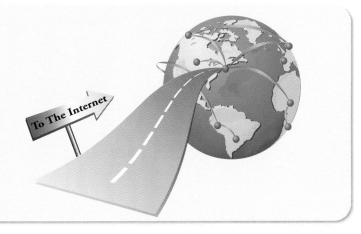

## INTERACTIVE

Instant messages are a very popular feature of commercial online services. You can instantly communicate with other people connected to the service by simply typing back and forth.

Most commercial online services also offer live, interactive events where members can exchange comments and questions with special guests, such as athletes and movie stars.

## MEMBER NAMES

Most commercial online services allow you to use a member name to identify yourself on the service. You use this name to log onto the service and to identify yourself in e-mail messages, discussion group messages and chat rooms. You can usually create a member name for each member of your family.

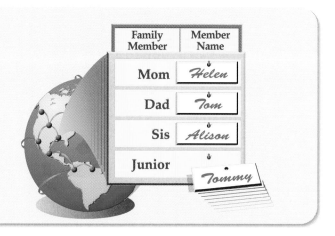

| Family Member | Member Name |
|---------------|-------------|
| Mom | Helen |
| Dad | Tom |
| Sis | Alison |
| Junior | Tommy |

## ACCESS FOR CHILDREN

Many commercial online services offer easy-to-use software that lets children access information on the online service and the Internet. Children can have fun exploring the Internet and meeting new friends. Parents can set restrictions on their accounts so their children will not be able to access offensive material on the Internet.

## CUSTOMER SUPPORT

Setting up a connection to a commercial online service is relatively easy. Online services usually provide good customer support for any questions you may have. Customer support should be available in the evenings and on weekends, as well as during business hours.

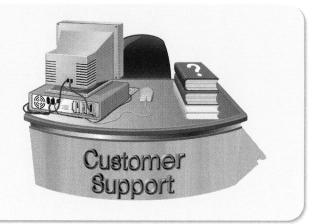

## COST

Most commercial online services let you try their service free of charge for a limited time. After the trial period, most online services offer a certain number of hours per month for a set fee.

If you exceed the total number of hours, you are usually charged for every extra hour you use the online service.

## PREMIUM SERVICES

Some commercial online services offer premium services, such as news services, that you can use for an additional fee. Make sure you are aware of how much you will be charged to use a premium service.

## WORLDWIDE ACCESS

Many commercial online services are available in most countries throughout the world. This makes online services ideal for people who travel frequently but still need access to services such as e-mail. Many businesses use commercial online services to communicate between offices located in different parts of the world.

# CONNECT TO THE INTERNET AT WORK

Many companies have their computer networks connected to the Internet. You may be able to use your computer at work to access the Internet.

## RESTRICTIONS

Most companies connected to the Internet do not offer access to all the features available on the Internet. Companies may restrict the type of information employees are allowed to access or may allow employees only to use the Internet to exchange e-mail. Check with your company's network administrator to find out which areas of the Internet you can access.

## CONNECT FROM HOME

Many companies allow employees to use a computer with a modem to access the company network from home. If the company network is connected to the Internet, employees may also be able to use the company network to access the Internet from home.

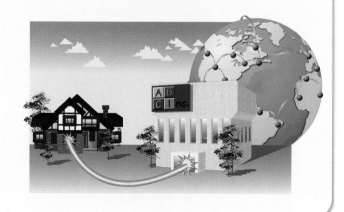

# CONNECT TO THE INTERNET AT SCHOOL

Many people access the Internet for the first time while they are at school. Schools have been connected to the Internet since the Internet first began.

## ELEMENTARY AND HIGH SCHOOLS

Most schools that allow students to access the Internet also provide instruction for students on how to use the Internet. Most schools have restrictions on the types of information students can access. Some schools also require students to sign a contract stating that they will not attempt to access inappropriate material.

## COLLEGES AND UNIVERSITIES

Many colleges and universities provide students and teachers with access to the Internet. Students may be able to use the school's computers or use their own computer to connect to the Internet through a school account.

Some colleges and universities limit Internet access. For example, students may be able to access the Internet for only a specific number of hours each week or only at certain times of the day.

# INTERNET CONNECTION TERMS

There are several terms you need to understand before connecting your computer to the Internet.

## ACCESS NUMBER

An access number is the phone number you dial to connect to your Internet access provider. You should try to make sure the access number is a local call. Otherwise, you may have to pay long distance charges for the time you spend on the Internet.

## CONNECTIONS

When you use a modem and phone line to connect to your Internet access provider, you use a dial-up connection.

When you use a high-speed connection, your computer is connected to the Internet 24-hours per day. You do not have to establish a dial-up connection to your access provider each time you want to connect to the Internet.

## SERVER

A server is a computer that stores information many people can access. Most of the information available on the Internet is stored on servers. A server usually has a name that indicates what type of information it stores. For example, the name of a server that stores e-mail messages usually starts with "mail."

## TCP/IP

To exchange files and information on the Internet, each computer on the Internet must use the same language. Transmission Control Protocol/Internet Protocol (TCP/IP) is the language used by computers to transfer information over the Internet.

## IP ADDRESS

Every computer connected to the Internet is identified by a unique number, called an Internet Protocol (IP) address. The IP address is made up of four different numbers separated by periods, such as 254.234.123.65

**Domain Name**

Since IP numbers are hard to remember, most computers also have a name, such as "company.com," which is easy to understand. When connecting to a computer, you can type the IP address or the name of the computer.

# INTERNET TELEVISION TERMINALS

**An Internet television terminal is an electronic device that allows you to access information on the Internet using your television.**

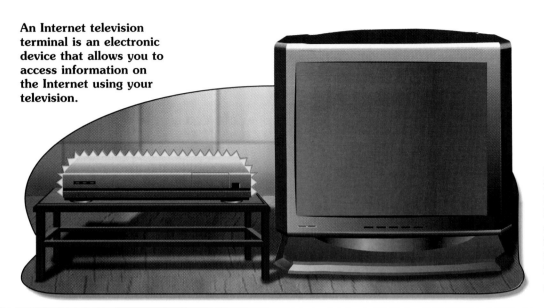

Internet television terminals are also known as set-top boxes. You can find out more about Internet television terminals from WebTV at the following Web site:

www.webtv.net

## TELEVISION FEATURES

Most Internet television terminals allow you to watch a television program while you are browsing the Web. This allows you to use hyperlinks to visit Web pages and chat rooms related to the current program. You can also use an Internet television terminal to view television program listings several days in advance and search for programs you want to watch.

## E-MAIL SERVICES

Internet television terminals allow you to send and receive e-mail messages using your television and a keyboard. You can buy a wireless keyboard so you can sit at a comfortable distance from the television while you type your messages.

## SOFTWARE

Internet television terminals include the software you need to access the Internet. Each terminal has programs that allow you to browse the World Wide Web and exchange e-mail. The programs used in the terminal can often be updated on the Internet.

## MODEM

Most Internet television terminals have a built-in modem with a speed of 56 Kbps. Before you can use the terminal, you have to connect the terminal to a phone line. When you use the terminal to access the Internet, the terminal automatically dials a number and connects you to the Internet access provider.

## DISPLAY

Some Web pages that are displayed on the television screen may not look as sharp as when viewed on a computer monitor. Computer monitors offer higher resolutions and more colors than most television screens.

## REMOTE CONTROL

Most Internet television terminals come equipped with a remote control. You can use the remote control instead of a mouse while browsing the World Wide Web.

## CHAPTER 3

# The World Wide Web

*Do you want to learn more about the World Wide Web? This chapter introduces you to the Web and what it has to offer.*

# INTRODUCTION TO THE WEB

**The World Wide Web is part of the Internet. The Web consists of a huge collection of documents stored on computers around the world.**

The World Wide Web is also referred to as the Web, WWW or W3.

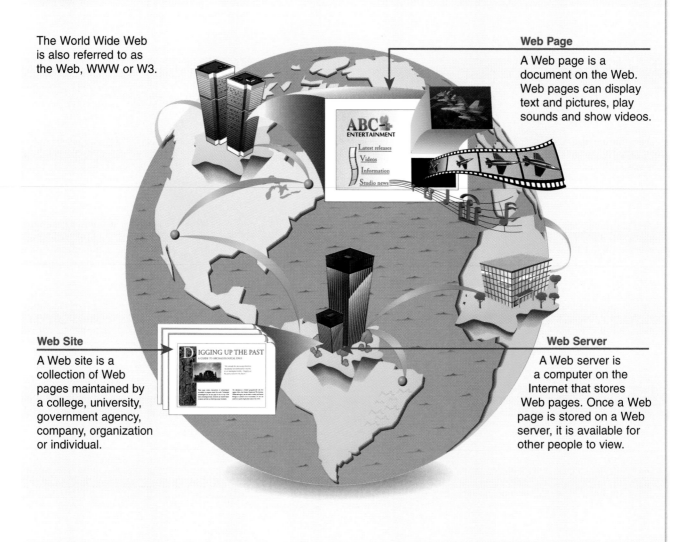

## Web Page

A Web page is a document on the Web. Web pages can display text and pictures, play sounds and show videos.

## Web Site

A Web site is a collection of Web pages maintained by a college, university, government agency, company, organization or individual.

## Web Server

A Web server is a computer on the Internet that stores Web pages. Once a Web page is stored on a Web server, it is available for other people to view.

## URL

Each Web page has a unique address, called a URL (Uniform Resource Locator). You can instantly display any Web page if you know its URL.

A Web page URL starts with **http** (HyperText Transfer Protocol) and usually contains the **computer name**, **directory name** and **name of the Web page**.

## HYPERLINKS

Web pages contain highlighted text or images, called hyperlinks, that connect to other pages on the Web. Hyperlinks allow you to easily move through a vast amount of information by jumping from one Web page to another. You can select a hyperlink to jump to a Web page located on the same computer or on a computer across the city, country or world.

Hyperlinks are also referred to as links.

You can easily identify text hyperlinks in a Web page because they appear underlined and in color.

# WEB BROWSERS

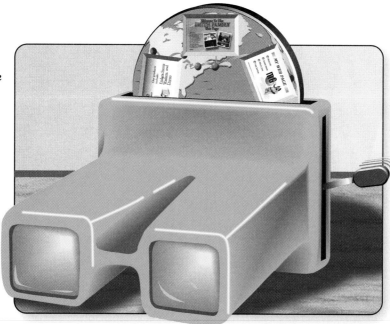

A Web browser is a program that lets you view and explore information on the World Wide Web.

Two popular Web browsers are Microsoft Internet Explorer and Netscape Navigator. For more information on these Web browsers, see pages 44 and 45.

## HTML SUPPORT

Web browsers display Web pages, which are documents created using a computer language called HyperText Markup Language (HTML). Each new version of HTML allows Web pages to use more features, such as multimedia and security. If a Web browser does not support the latest version of HTML, the browser will not be able to use the newest features. Version 4.0 is the latest version of HTML.

## BETA VERSION

A beta version of a Web browser is an early version of the program that is not quite ready for release. Many companies let people use and test the beta version of their Web browser before releasing the official version. Beta versions of Web browsers sometimes contain errors.

## HOME PAGE

The home page is the Web page that appears each time you start your Web browser. You can choose any page on the Web as your home page. Choose a home page that provides a good starting point for exploring the Web.

## BOOKMARKS

Most Web browsers have a feature called bookmarks or favorites. This feature lets you store the addresses of Web pages you frequently visit. Bookmarks save you from having to remember and constantly retype your favorite Web page addresses.

## HISTORY LIST

When browsing through pages on the World Wide Web, it can be difficult to keep track of the locations of pages you have visited. Most Web browsers include a history list that allows you to quickly return to a Web page you recently visited.

## NAVIGATION BUTTONS

Most Web browsers provide buttons to help you move through information on the Web. You can move back and forward through Web pages you have viewed or stop the transfer of a Web page that is taking a long time to appear.

# MICROSOFT INTERNET EXPLORER

**Microsoft Internet Explorer is currently the most popular Web browser.**

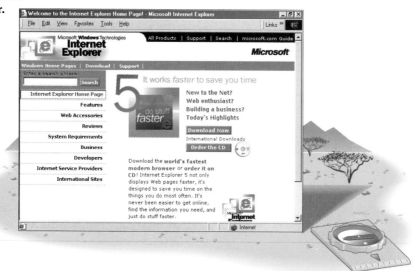

Internet Explorer comes with the Windows 98 operating system. You can also get Internet Explorer free of charge at the following Web site:

www.microsoft.com/ie

## EASY TO USE

Internet Explorer was created by the same company that created the Windows operating systems, so the look and feel of Internet Explorer is very similar to the look and feel of other Windows programs. If you are familiar with other Windows programs, you should find the Web browser easy to learn and use.

## INTERNET EXPLORER FEATURES

Internet Explorer offers many features that help you efficiently work on the Web. For example, Internet Explorer's Search feature can help you quickly locate information you are looking for. You can also customize Internet Explorer to suit your needs.

# NETSCAPE NAVIGATOR

**Netscape Navigator is a popular Web browser. Netscape Navigator was one of the first Web browsers used on the Internet.**

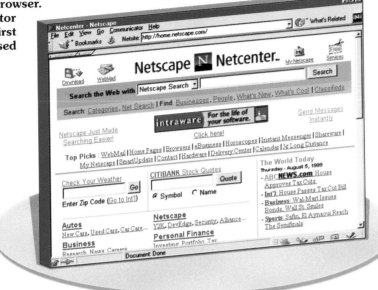

Netscape Navigator includes many features that can improve the time you spend browsing through information on the Web.

## VERSATILE

Navigator is available for computers running many different operating systems, including Windows, Macintosh and Unix. You can get Navigator as a separate program or as part of the Netscape Communicator suite, which includes several other useful programs for the Internet. You can obtain Netscape Navigator free of charge at the following Web site:

www.netscape.com

## NETSCAPE EXTENSIONS

HyperText Markup Language (HTML) is the name of the programming language used to create Web pages. Netscape continually makes improvements, called Netscape extensions, to HTML. These improvements allow Web pages to include features such as enhanced video and sound.

# ERROR MESSAGES

An error message appears when your Web browser cannot properly display a Web page.

## COMMON ERROR MESSAGES

### 403 FORBIDDEN

The 403 Forbidden error message appears when you try to open a Web page you do not have permission to access. You cannot view the Web page without permission.

### 404 NOT FOUND

The 404 Not Found error message appears when your Web browser cannot find the Web page you specified. The Web page may have moved or the name of the Web page may have changed.

### SERVER NOT FOUND

The Server Not Found error message appears when your Web browser cannot access the server you specified. A server is a computer that stores information on the Internet. The server may be busy, temporarily not working or may not exist.

When an error message appears on your screen, you can try one of the following options to display the Web page you want to view.

## OPTIONS

### CHECK FOR TYPING ERRORS

If you typed the Web page address, you should check the address for typing errors. Typing errors are the main reason a Web page will not appear.

### TRY AGAIN

Sometimes your Web browser cannot open a Web page on the first try. You can try clicking the Refresh or Reload button in your Web browser to try opening the Web page again.

### TRY DURING OFF-PEAK HOURS

You can try opening the Web page later. The best time to try opening a popular Web page is during off-peak hours, such as nights and weekends. Fewer people browse the Web at these times.

### CHECK YOUR INTERNET CONNECTION

If you cannot open any Web pages, make sure you are still connected to the Internet. Sometimes a disturbance on the line can disconnect your computer.

# CHILDREN AND THE WEB

**Children should be carefully monitored when using the Web.**

Most of the information on the Web is meant to educate or entertain people, but some of the information is inappropriate for children.

## TYPES OF INAPPROPRIATE INFORMATION

### PICTURES

There are many sites on the Web that display pictures meant for adult users. Most adult-oriented sites require verification that users are adults, but the sites often display sample pictures on the first page of the Web site.

### TEXT FILES

There are many text files on the Web describing everything from causing mischief at school to making explosives. These types of text files often appeal to teenagers and generally do not have any restrictions on who can access the text files.

## WAYS TO RESTRICT ACCESS

### ADULT SUPERVISION

Constant adult supervision is the best way to ensure that children do not access inappropriate information on the Web. Before a child spends time browsing the Web, you should discuss the purpose of the session with the child and set ground rules.

You may want to keep the computer in the family room or kitchen so you can monitor the information your children access.

### WEB BROWSER RESTRICTIONS

Some Web browsers have built-in restrictions. Users can view only sites that have been approved by a rating system similar to the system used to rate films. You can decide which rating level is appropriate for your children.

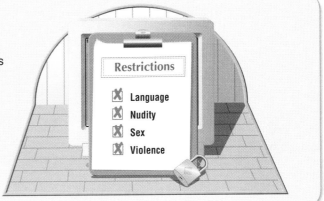

### RESTRICTION PROGRAMS

There are many programs available that allow you to restrict the information your children can access on the Web and most areas of the Internet.

You can find restriction programs at the following Web sites:

**Net Nanny**

www.netnanny.com

**Cyber Patrol**

www.cyberpatrol.com

# WEB PORTALS

A Web portal is a Web site that provides an excellent starting point for exploring the Internet.

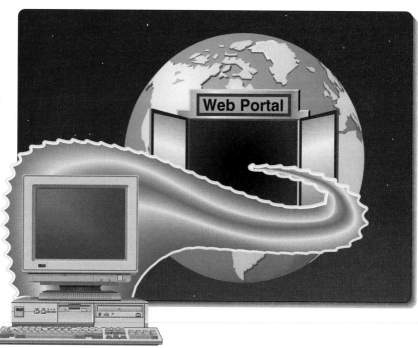

You can find popular Web portals at the following Web sites:

www.yahoo.com

www.go.com

www.lycos.com

## CONTENT CATEGORIES

Web portals allow you to browse through categories, such as business or sports, to find information that interests you. Web portals also let you type a word or phrase to quickly search for information on the Web.

## NEWS

Most Web portals provide a variety of up-to-date news headlines, as well as sports scores and stock quotes. You can select a news headline to read a full article on the news item.

## SHOPPING

Many Web portals provide access to online shopping. You can buy anything from clothing and sports equipment to books and gardening tools.

### FREE E-MAIL

Web portals usually offer free e-mail services, which allow you to send and receive e-mail from any computer that has access to the Web.

### CHAT

Web portals often offer chat services that allow you to instantly communicate with people around the world.

### PEOPLE SEARCH

Most Web portals allow you to search the white pages directory to find telephone numbers and addresses. Many portals also let you search for e-mail addresses.

### MAPS

Many Web portals offer maps and driving directions. For example, you can find the distance and best route between two addresses.

### GAMES

Most Web portals allow you to play games, such as chess or crossword puzzles. You can play against the computer or against other people visiting the portal.

### CUSTOMIZE

You can customize many Web portals to display the information you want. For example, you could customize a Web portal to display the weather forecast for your area.

# SECURITY ON THE WEB

There are several ways to ensure the personal information you send over the Internet is secure.

Many people feel it is unsafe to transmit credit card numbers over the Internet. In fact, sending a credit card number to a Web page can be safer than giving the number to an unknown person over the phone.

## SECURE WEB PAGES

Secure Web pages work with Web browsers to create an almost unbreakable security system that protects information you send over the Internet. When you send information, the information may pass through many computers before reaching its destination. If you are not connected to a secure Web page, other people on the Internet may be able to view the information you transfer.

### Visit Secure Web Pages

The address of a secure Web page usually starts with **https** rather than **http**.

When you visit a secure Web page, your Web browser will usually display a lock or key on the screen to indicate that the Web page is secure. Many Web browsers also display a dialog box alerting you that you are about to view a secure Web page.

## COOKIE

A cookie is a small text file stored on your computer. The information in the cookie is used by a Web site to keep track of people who access the site. For example, when you visit a Web site, the site may create a cookie to store your name. The next time you visit the Web site, your Web browser will access the cookie stored on your computer and display your name on the Web page.

### Sharing a Computer

If you share a computer with other people at work, you should be careful of cookies stored on the computer. For example, if you use the computer to purchase an item at a Web site, your credit card information may be stored as a cookie. If a co-worker then uses the same computer to visit the same Web site, the co-worker could purchase items using your credit card information. Many Web browsers allow you to turn off the use of cookies.

## FIREWALL

A firewall is a program that restricts information passing between two networks. Many organizations use firewalls to prevent unauthorized individuals on the Internet from accessing a private network. If your company uses a firewall, you may need to contact your system administrator for help in accessing the Internet from work.

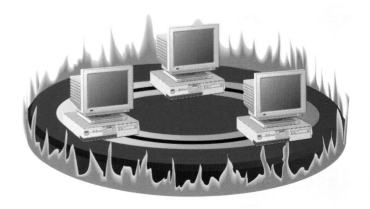

# SHOPPING ON THE WEB

**You can buy products and services on the Web without ever leaving your desk.**

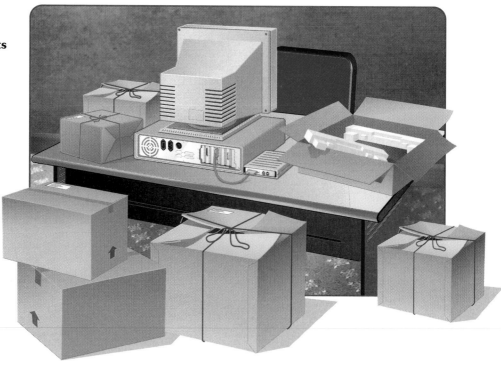

## PRODUCTS AVAILABLE

There are thousands of products you can buy on the Web, such as clothing, office supplies, computer programs and food. The Web is also a great source for purchasing rare items, such as out-of-print books and collectibles.

## SHOPPING CARTS

Like shopping at a traditional store, many Web sites allow you to place all the items you want to purchase in a shopping cart. The shopping cart stores information about the items you have selected while you continue browsing through the Web site. When you finish shopping, you can purchase all the items in the shopping cart at once.

**Your Shopping Cart**

| Item | Store | Options | Unit Price | Quantity | Subtotal | |
|------|-------|---------|-----------|----------|----------|---|
| Fax Machine #4521748 | electronics.world | | 329.97 | 1 | 329.97 | Remove |
| Camera #6854329 | electronics.world | | 139.97 | 1 | 139.97 | Remove |
| | | | | **Total:** | 469.94 | |

Place Order   Keep Shopping   Update Cart

## SHOPPING CONSIDERATIONS

### DELIVERY

When you buy a product on the Web, you can usually have the product delivered to your door. Most companies charge for delivery, which can greatly increase the price of a product. Consider the delivery charges involved before purchasing a product.

### RETURNS

Keep in mind that you may be ordering from a company located anywhere in the world. This can make it more difficult to return a product you do not find suitable. You should check the return policy before ordering any products.

### CREDIT CARDS

Many people feel it is unsafe to transmit credit card numbers over the Internet. In fact, sending a credit card number to a secure Web page is safer than giving the number to an unknown person over the phone. For information on secure Web pages, see page 52.

## ADVANTAGES OF SHOPPING ON THE WEB

### CONVENIENCE

Shopping on the Web can be more convenient than shopping in traditional stores. You can shop on the Web 24 hours a day, seven days a week.

If you live in a rural area, there may not be a wide variety of stores nearby. The Web gives you access to products from around the world.

### UP-TO-DATE INFORMATION

Most Web sites offer more up-to-date information about products and prices than catalogs and flyers. You can also use the Web to find reviews and ratings of the products you want to buy. This allows you to make an informed decision before making your purchase.

### RESEARCH COMPANIES

When shopping on the Web, you can use the resources on the Internet to find information about the companies you are purchasing from. You can find opinions of other customers and information about the reputation of the company.

### ONE-STOP SHOPPING

Many Web sites allow you to purchase many different types of products in one place. You can purchase books, clothing, electronics and gifts all at the same Web site.

You can find one-stop shopping at the following Web sites:

www.shopping.com

www.imall.com

### LOW PRICES

Prices for products sold on the Web are generally lower than prices in traditional stores because companies do not have overhead costs, such as rent and salespeople. Many stores on the Web also give discounts when you make a purchase.

You can even find electronic coupons for many items at the following Web sites:

www.couponsurfer.com

www.coolsavings.com

### COMPARISON SHOPPING

You can use the Web to compare products and prices. There are many Web sites that will do comparison shopping for you. When you search for the product you want, the Web site will display a list of matching products with prices and links for ordering.

You can find comparison shopping tools at the following Web sites:

www.bottomdollar.com

www.shopfind.com

# AUCTIONS ON THE WEB

You can find auctions on the Web where you can bid on products such as computers, jewelry, gifts and much more.

## TYPES OF AUCTIONS

### PERSON-TO-PERSON

Person-to-person auctions provide a meeting place for buyers and sellers. Many person-to-person auctions are like giant flea markets and are ideal for finding rare items.

You can find person-to-person auctions at the following Web sites:

www.ebay.com

www.auctionuniverse.com

### MERCHANT

Businesses use merchant auctions to offer their merchandise to the public. Merchant auctions often offer over-stocked or refurbished products, such as computers, housewares and sporting goods.

You can find merchant auctions at the following Web sites:

www.ubid.com

www.onsale.com

### TRADITIONAL AUCTIONS

Some traditional auction houses, such as Sotheby's, are beginning to offer auctions on the Web. These auctions specialize in fine art, antiques, collectibles and jewelry.

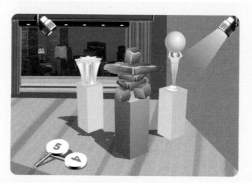

You can find the Sotheby's Web site at:

www.sothebys.com

## AUCTION FORMATS

### DUTCH AUCTIONS

In a Dutch auction, a seller offers multiple quantities of an item and specifies the minimum bid they will accept. Each bidder specifies the quantity of the item they want and the price they are willing to pay. The items go to the people who bid on the highest quantity at the best price.

### RESERVE AUCTION

In a Reserve auction, a seller sets the minimum price they will accept for an item. If the minimum price is not reached, the seller can remove the item from the auction.

## BIDDING CONSIDERATIONS

### COMPARE PRICES

Before bidding on a product, browse the Web to see what companies are charging for similar products. You may be able to buy the product for a lower price.

### CHECK SHIPPING FEES

Shipping fees can greatly increase the price of a product. Consider the shipping fees involved before bidding on a product.

### ALL SALES ARE FINAL

All sales are final on auction Web sites. At a merchant auction, if you win the bidding, your credit card is charged immediately.

# TRAVEL ON THE WEB

The Web is a great resource for planning a trip. You can book flights, rent cars, reserve hotel rooms and much more.

## INFORMATION

Travel Web sites are great sources of travel information. You can get information about a city you want to visit, such as local attractions, restaurants or a calendar of events for the time of your trip.

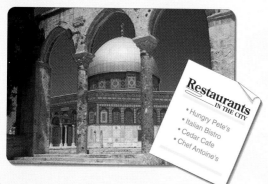

You can also find reviews written by other travelers and tips to make your trip more enjoyable.

## POPULAR TRAVEL WEB SITES

There are many travel sites on the Web. The following Web sites provide an excellent starting point for planning a trip:

www.expedia.com

www.previewtravel.com

www.travelocity.com

## LOW PRICES

Prices on the Web are generally lower than prices in traditional travel agencies because the Web sites do not have overhead costs, such as rent. You can also use travel Web sites to compare prices and ensure you get the best deal. Most travel Web sites offer discount hotel and car rental plans.

## PRICE BIDS

Some Web sites allow you to specify the price you want to spend for a flight or hotel room. The Web site then contacts companies to find one that will accept your price. You can find this feature at the following Web site:

www.priceline.com

## CONVENIENCE

Making your travel plans on the Web can be more convenient than using a traditional travel agent. You can book flights and reserve hotel rooms on the Web 24 hours a day, seven days a week. Travel Web sites also help with your planning by offering many useful tools in one location. For example, you can find maps, currency converters and up-to-date weather reports at most travel Web sites.

# BANKING ON THE WEB

Many banks allow you to access your banking information over the Web. You can pay bills, check your account balances and transfer money between accounts.

## SECURITY

Banking information is one of the most confidential types of information. Banks use secure Web sites to keep your information private. For information on secure Web sites, see page 52.

Some banks may require you to download a component that will upgrade the security of your Web browser before you can perform banking transactions on the Web.

## CONVENIENCE

You can access your banking information when it is convenient for you–24 hours a day, seven days a week. You can also use the Web to schedule your bill payments in advance. This is useful if you are going on vacation or away on business.

Paying Invoice...

## RECEIVE YOUR BILLS ONLINE

Many companies now deliver bills over the Internet instead of through the mail. Just like a traditional bill, when you receive a bill online, you can see the payment due date, the amount due and even the detail of the bill. Receiving and paying bills on the Internet can help reduce the time you spend paying your bills each month.

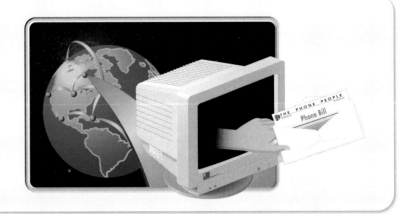

## PERSONAL FINANCE PROGRAMS

Many people use personal finance programs to organize their finances. Most banks also work with these programs. Instead of entering your banking transactions each month, you can transfer the information from your bank's Web site to the program on your computer.

You can find personal finance programs at the following Web sites:

**Intuit Quicken**

www.intuit.com/quicken_store

**Microsoft Money**

www.microsoft.com/money

## FINANCIAL SERVICES

Many banks provide financial services on their Web sites. For example, you can apply for a mortgage or a loan on the Web. You can also use an online calculator to estimate your monthly mortgage or loan payments.

# INVESTING ON THE WEB

You can buy and sell stocks, bonds and mutual funds on the Web. The Web can also help you learn more about investing.

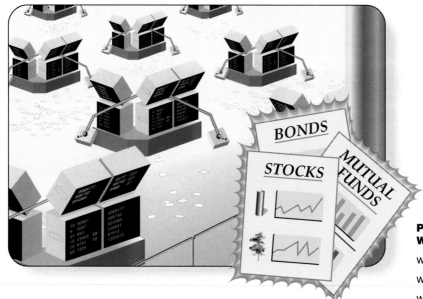

**Popular Investment Web Sites**

www.etrade.com

www.ameritrade.com

www.schwab.com

## ADVANTAGES OF INVESTING ON THE WEB

### WIDE VARIETY OF INFORMATION

The Web offers information on investing, daily market bulletins, real-time stock quotes and detailed financial information about companies. Some investment Web sites require you to pay a subscription fee to access the information. You can find information at the following Web sites:

www.techstocks.com

www.thestreet.com

www.fool.com

### CREATE PORTFOLIOS

You can create several investment portfolios and monitor their progress on the Web. Many investment Web sites also let you create an imaginary stock portfolio that you can use to practice trading stocks. This allows you to fully understand stock trading on the Web before you begin investing your own money.

## CONSIDERATIONS FOR INVESTING ON THE WEB

When buying and selling stocks on the Web, you should keep in mind that your orders may not be filled immediately. Delays can occur when transferring information over the Internet, which can be costly since the price of stock can change in only a few minutes.

## TYPES OF STOCK ORDERS

The most common types of stock orders are market orders and limit orders. A market order is usually filled as soon as the online broker receives the order. This type of order can be costly if the price changes before the order reaches the broker.

A limit order allows you to specify the maximum price you will pay for stock or the minimum price that you will sell the stock for.

## DAYTRADING

Daytrading refers to buying and selling stocks from minute to minute in an attempt to make money quickly. Daytrading involves more risk than long-term investing, but the amount of up-to-the-minute investment information available on the Web makes daytrading much easier.

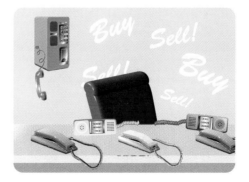

# EMPLOYMENT ON THE WEB

There are thousands of Web sites that can help you find a job.

## CAREER PLANNING

There are many Web sites that can help you find the right career. You can access self-assessment questionnaires, quizzes to evaluate your skills and a listing of the qualifications you need to get your dream job. You can also find tips on how to find a job, how to write a résumé and how to handle job interviews.

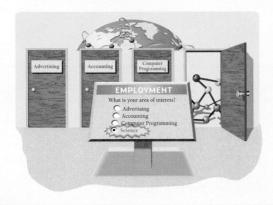

## COMPANIES

Many companies have a Web page that provides information about the company and available positions within the company. Most companies provide an e-mail or mailing address you can use to apply for a position. A company's Web site is also a good way to find information about the company before going for an interview.

## JOB SEARCH

### SEARCH FOR JOBS

Most job search Web sites allow you to search for jobs in a specific city or country. You can also search for job openings in a particular company. When searching for jobs, you can specify a category of jobs you are interested in, such as administrative or manufacturing, or enter a keyword, such as chef or editor.

Popular job search Web sites include the following:

www.careermosaic.com

www.hotjobs.com

www.monster.com

### POST YOUR RÉSUMÉ

Many job search Web sites allow you to store your résumé on the Web site for potential employers to review. Some Web sites also allow you to specify which companies you do not want to be able to view your résumé.

### MONITOR NEW JOB OPENINGS

Some Web sites allow you to specify your requirements for a job. The Web site will then monitor new job postings and notify you when there is a job opening matching your requirements.

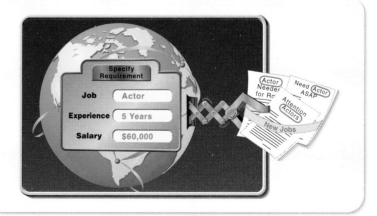

# EDUCATION ON THE WEB

There are many resources on the Web that can help you learn about new subjects. You can even take university courses and other classes on the Web.

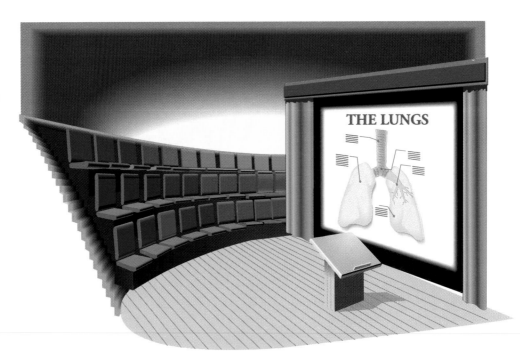

## PRODUCT SUPPORT

Many companies use the Web to provide product support for their customers. This means that customers do not have to use older methods, such as the telephone or regular mail, to get product support. You can also often get product manuals and specifications on the Web.

## REFERENCE TOOLS

There are many types of reference tools available on the Web. You can find dictionaries for many different languages, translation services, encyclopedias, books of famous quotations and much more. Most reference tools on the Web are available free of charge.

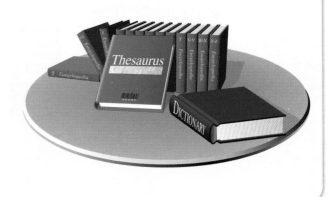

### STEP-BY-STEP INSTRUCTION

Documents on the Web can be joined together in a specific order using hyperlinks. This makes the Web very useful for step-by-step instructional guides. Each step can be displayed as a single document. You can move through the steps one at a time, at your own pace. You can also print out each document and use the pages for reference later.

### SCHOOLS

Many schools and universities offer courses you can complete using the Internet. The school or university will often make lecture notes and diagrams for the course available on the Web. You can also often send projects and essays to the instructor by electronic mail.

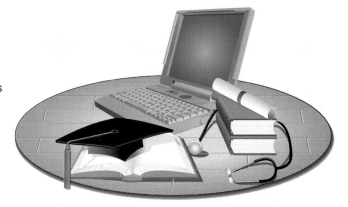

### LIVE INSTRUCTION

Sound and video can transfer over the Internet. Students will soon be able to use their computers at home to view and participate in classes taking place at a school or university. This is useful for students who are ill or who live far away from the school.

# NEWS ON THE WEB

**You can use the Web to keep up-to-date on the latest news stories.**

Web-based news is ideal if you have specific interests. For example, you can quickly access news stories about your favorite sports team.

## NEWSPAPERS AND TELEVISION NETWORKS

Newspapers often provide news stories and images on the Web. Many television networks also have Web sites where they offer news stories with sound and video clips. You can find popular newspapers and television networks at the following Web sites:

www.nytimes.com          www.cnn.com

www.washingtonpost.com          www.bloomberg.com

## BREAKING NEWS

You can access the latest breaking news stories at the same time as most other mainstream news organizations. This allows you to keep on top of the news as it happens. You can find links to many different news sources at the following Web site:

www.drudgereport.com

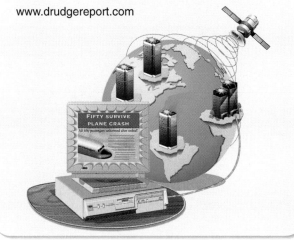

The Web is an excellent source of research material. You can find reports, statistics, directories and much more.

## DATABASES

Many schools, companies and organizations on the Web allow people to access information stored in their databases. A database is a large collection of information. You can find databases containing information such as company directories and registered patents.

## RESEARCH FIRMS

Many companies and organizations on the Web allow people to access information such as surveys, market research and consumer reports. There are several popular research firms on the Web.

You can find research firms at the following Web sites:

www.forrester.com

www.gallup.com

## COST

Some Web sites require you to pay a fee to access the information available. You may be able to access a small amount of information free of charge. This allows you to try out the Web site before paying to access the information.

## CHAPTER 4

# Web Page Enhancements

*Are you wondering what makes Web pages so exciting? Read this chapter to find out about sound and video on Web pages and much more.*

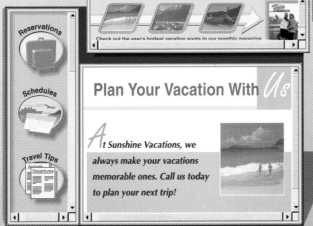

# INTRODUCTION TO MULTIMEDIA

**Multimedia is an effective way of attracting attention to information on a Web page.**

Multimedia is a combination of text, images, sound and video or animation. Many companies that advertise on the Web use multimedia to sell their products and services.

TRANSFER TIME

Some files take a while to transfer to your computer. A Web page usually shows the size of a file to give you an indication of how long the file will take to transfer.

| | File Size | | Time |
|---|---|---|---|
| Bytes | Kilobytes (KB) | Megabytes (MB) | (estimated) |
| 10,000,000 | 10,000 | 10 | 25 minutes |
| 5,000,000 | 5,000 | 5 | 12 minutes |
| 2,500,000 | 2,500 | 2.5 | 8 minutes |

Use this chart as a guide to determine how long a file will take to transfer to your computer.

This chart is based on transferring files with a 56 Kbps modem. A modem with a lower speed will transfer files more slowly than shown in the chart.

## TEXT

You can view documents on the Web, such as newspapers, magazines, plays, famous speeches and television show transcripts. Text transfers quickly to your computer, so you do not have to wait long to read text on a Web page.

## IMAGES

You can view images on the Web, such as album covers, pictures of celebrities and famous paintings.

## SOUND

You can listen to sound on the Web, such as TV theme songs, movie soundtracks, sound effects and historical speeches. You need a sound card and speakers to listen to sound on the Web.

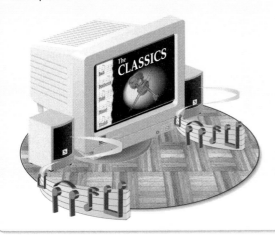

## VIDEO AND ANIMATION

You can view video and animation on the Web, such as movie clips, cartoons and interviews with celebrities.

# SOUNDS

**Web pages can include sounds to entertain and inform you.**

Your computer must have sound capabilities to play sounds.

## SOUNDS ON THE WEB

Entertainment is the most popular reason for including sounds on Web pages. You can listen to sound clips from television shows, movies and famous speeches. Companies that sell music CDs and audiotapes also often include sounds to let you listen to samples of their products.

## WHERE TO FIND SOUNDS

There are many Web pages that provide sounds. You can listen to the sounds on the Web page or copy a sound to your own computer for later use. Make sure you have permission to use any sounds you obtain on the Web.

You can find sounds at the following Web sites:

soundamerica.com          www.wavcentral.com

www.mp3.com

## TYPES OF SOUNDS

There are several types of sounds on the Web. The most popular type of sound is Wave. You can determine the type of a sound by the characters that appear after the period in the sound file name (example: birdchirp.wav).

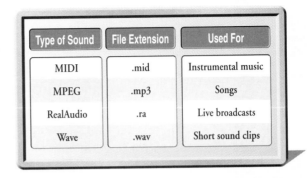

| Type of Sound | File Extension | Used For |
|---|---|---|
| MIDI | .mid | Instrumental music |
| MPEG | .mp3 | Songs |
| RealAudio | .ra | Live broadcasts |
| Wave | .wav | Short sound clips |

Type:
MPEG

Size:
2.5 MB

Time:
3 mins

## READ DESCRIPTIONS

Most Web pages provide a short description of each sound you can listen to, including the sound type, size and length of time the sound will play. You can use this information to decide if you want to play the sound. When reading descriptions, keep in mind that large sound files can take a long time to transfer to your computer.

## SOUND QUALITY

Several factors can affect the quality of sound on the Web. For example, small sound files may have been compressed to transfer faster over the Web and may have lower quality than larger sound files. Some types of sounds may also provide better quality than others. For example, an MPEG file usually has better quality than a Wave file.

Wave

MPEG

Web pages can include video to educate and entertain, as well as advertise products.

Your computer must have sound capabilities to play the sound included with a video.

## VIDEO ON THE WEB

Web pages can include videos to display eye-catching visual effects, movie clips, animation, home videos, TV broadcasts or demonstrations of a product or service. Videos are also useful for providing information about a company or organization.

## WHERE TO FIND VIDEO

There are many Web pages that allow you to view videos and copy videos to your own computer. Make sure you have permission to use any videos you obtain on the Web. You can find videos at the following Web sites:

www.jurassicpunk.com     videolinks.interspeed.net

moviecentral.hypermart.net

## TYPES OF VIDEO

There are several types of video on the Web. You can determine the type of a video by the characters that appear after the period in the video file name (example: plane.avi). Some Web browsers can play only certain types of video, while other Web browsers cannot play any video types.

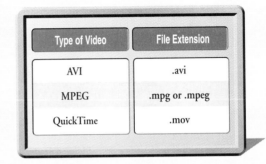

| Type of Video | File Extension |
|---|---|
| AVI | .avi |
| MPEG | .mpg or .mpeg |
| QuickTime | .mov |

## READ DESCRIPTIONS

Most Web pages provide a short description of each video you can view, including the type, size and length of time the video will play. Video files tend to be the largest files on the Web. Keep in mind that large video files can take a long time to transfer to your computer.

## VIDEO QUALITY

Video files on the Web are often compressed so the files will transfer faster over the Web. The amount of compression can affect the quality of a video. If a video file is compressed too much, it may lower the quality of the video.

# FORMS

**Web pages can include forms that allow you to send information to the person or company that created the Web pages.**

Forms can be used to gather information about people who visit Web pages. Many companies also include forms that allow you to purchase products and services on the Web.

## HOW FORMS WORK

### GATHER INFORMATION

You can enter information and select options on a form. When you finish entering information into a form, you can click a "Submit" button on the form to transfer the information to a Web server.

### PROCESS INFORMATION

When a Web server receives the information you entered into a form, the server runs a program that processes the information. The Web server then prepares the results for the person or company that created the Web pages.

Frames split a Web
browser window into
sections. Each section
displays a different
Web page.

## REASONS FOR USING FRAMES

### BANNERS

A frame can display a banner
that remains on the screen as
you browse through the pages
in a Web site. Banners are
useful for displaying information
such as an advertisement or a
company logo.

### NAVIGATION

A frame can help you move
through Web pages and find
information of interest. For
example, a frame can display a
table of contents, navigational
tools or search tools that remain
on the screen at all times.

### SUPPORTING INFORMATION

A frame can display information
on the screen as you move
through the Web pages in a
Web site. This is ideal for
supporting information such
as copyright notices, footnotes
and references.

# TABLES

Tables display information on a Web page in an organized and attractive format.

## PARTS OF A TABLE

### Row

A row is a horizontal line of data.

### Column

A column is a vertical line of data.

### Cell

A cell is the area where a row and column intersect.

| Last Name | First Name | Street | City |
|-----------|------------|--------|------|
| Smith | John | 258 Linton Dr. | New York |
| Lang | Kristin | 50 Tree Lane | Boston |
| Oram | Derek | 68 Cracker Ave. | San Francisco |
| Gray | Russell | 401 Idon Dr. | Atlanta |
| Atherly | Peter | 47 Crosby Ave. | Las Vegas |
| Talbot | Mark | 26 Arnold Lane | Seattle |

## REASONS FOR USING TABLES

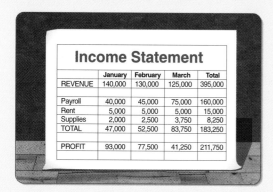

### Income Statement

|  | January | February | March | Total |
|--|---------|----------|-------|-------|
| REVENUE | 140,000 | 130,000 | 125,000 | 395,000 |
|  |  |  |  |  |
| Payroll | 40,000 | 45,000 | 75,000 | 160,000 |
| Rent | 5,000 | 5,000 | 5,000 | 15,000 |
| Supplies | 2,000 | 2,500 | 3,750 | 8,250 |
| TOTAL | 47,000 | 52,500 | 83,750 | 183,250 |
|  |  |  |  |  |
| PROFIT | 93,000 | 77,500 | 41,250 | 211,750 |

### Lists of Information

Tables provide a great way to neatly display lists of information such as financial data and price lists. Tables can display borders that separate each cell in the table to make the data easier to read.

### Control Web Page Layout

Tables are useful for organizing the placement of text and images on a Web page. For example, a table lets you neatly display an image between two paragraphs. Tables can also help you display information in columns like those found in a newspaper.

Web pages can include ActiveX controls to improve the appearance of the pages.

An ActiveX control is a program written using a programming language such as C++ or Visual Basic.

## REASONS FOR USING ACTIVEX CONTROLS

ActiveX controls allow you to listen to music and watch animation and video clips on the Web. Many Web pages use ActiveX controls to display drop down menus that provide a list of options. ActiveX controls are also used to include information in Web pages from popular programs such as Microsoft Word.

You can find examples of ActiveX controls at the following Web site:

www.download.com/PC/Activex

## OLDER WEB BROWSERS

Before viewing a Web page that includes ActiveX controls, you must have a Web browser that supports ActiveX controls, such as Microsoft Internet Explorer. Netscape Navigator and older Web browsers may need a plug-in to be able to use ActiveX controls. For information on plug-ins, see page 86.

# JAVA APPLETS

**Web pages can include Java applets to display animated and interactive information.**

A Java applet is a program written using the Java programming language.

## REASONS FOR USING JAVA APPLETS

### Entertainment

Java applets can make a Web page more entertaining by adding special effects such as rotating images, fireworks and animated text. Java applets can also allow you to play simple games or chat with other people viewing the same Web page. You can find examples of Java applets at the following Web site:

www.gamelan.com

### Information

Java applets are ideal for displaying information that constantly changes, such as stock market updates, the time, weather information and news headlines.

## OLDER WEB BROWSERS

Before you can view a Java applet on a Web page, you must have a Web browser that can run Java applets. Older Web browsers may not be able to run Java applets.

Web pages can include JavaScript to make the pages more interactive.

Although the names are similar, JavaScript and Java applets have very little in common.

## REASONS FOR USING JAVASCRIPT

JavaScript can display alert messages, offer drop down menus, open new windows and change images in response to mouse movements. JavaScript allows you to create dynamic Web pages, known as Dynamic HTML (DHTML). You can find examples of JavaScript at the following Web sites:

javascript.internet.com

www.javascripts.com

## OLDER WEB BROWSERS

Before you can view JavaScript on a Web page, you must have a Web browser that can run JavaScript. Older Web browsers may not be able to run JavaScript. If a Web browser cannot run JavaScript, the code for the JavaScript may appear on the Web page.

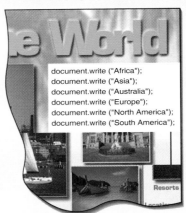

# WEB BROWSER PLUG-INS

Some Web browsers need special programs, called plug-ins, to display or play certain types of files on the Web. A plug-in performs tasks the Web browser cannot perform on its own.

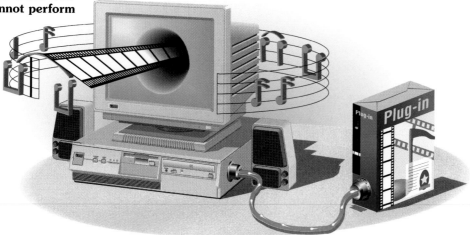

Plug-ins are also referred to as helper applications.

## WEB BROWSERS

Some Web browsers include several popular plug-ins. If your Web browser does not have the necessary plug-in to display or play a file on a Web page, the Web browser may present a dialog box telling you which plug-in you need.

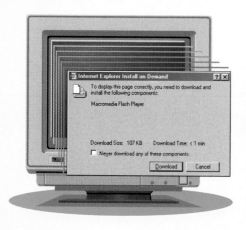

## GETTING PLUG-INS

If you want to display or play a file your Web browser cannot work with, you can download, or copy, the appropriate plug-in from the Web. Most plug-ins are offered free of charge. You can find a list of many popular plug-ins at the following Web site:

www.netscape.com/plugins

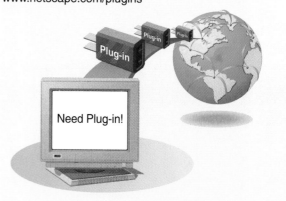

## POPULAR PLUG-INS

### ACROBAT READER

Acrobat Reader lets you view and print Portable Document Format (.pdf) files. This plug-in allows you to display books and magazines on your screen exactly as they appear in printed form. You can get Acrobat Reader at the following Web site:

www.adobe.com

### FLASH PLAYER

The Flash Player plug-in lets you view graphics and animation on the Web. Flash Player is often used for entertainment, such as animated cartoons. You can get Flash Player at the following Web site:

www.macromedia.com

### REALPLAYER

The RealPlayer plug-in lets you hear or view continuous sound or video on the Web. You can get RealPlayer at the following Web site:

www.real.com

### QUICKTIME

The QuickTime plug-in lets you watch videos and listen to a variety of sound formats on the Web. You can get QuickTime at the following Web site:

www.apple.com/quicktime

# STREAMING MULTIMEDIA

**Streaming multimedia is a system that lets you hear or view continuous sound or video on the Web.**

## HOW STREAMING MULTIMEDIA WORKS

Normally, when you transfer a sound or video file from the Web to your computer, you must wait for the entire file to transfer before you can play the sound or video. Streaming multimedia transfers sound and video files from the Web to a streaming multimedia player on your computer. The player plays the sound or video while the file is transferring to your computer.

## STREAMING MULTIMEDIA PLAYERS

You must have a streaming multimedia player to play streaming multimedia on the Web. You can find streaming multimedia players at the following Web sites:

**Microsoft Media Player**

www.microsoft.com/windows/mediaplayer

**RealNetworks RealPlayer**

www.real.com

## USING STREAMING MULTIMEDIA

### LIVE CONCERTS AND SPORTING EVENTS

Many musicians broadcast their concerts on the Web. You can experience the music live without leaving your desk. You can also watch live sporting events, such as baseball games or tennis matches, on your computer.

You can find concerts, sporting events and even television programs at the following Web site:

www.broadcast.com

### EDUCATION

Some colleges and distance education classes now offer course materials on the Web. Streaming multimedia allows you to listen to live lectures or watch instructional videos on your computer.

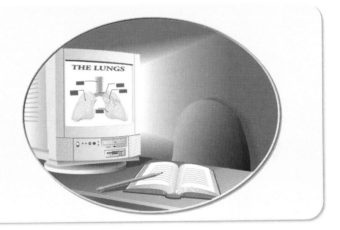

### RADIO PROGRAMS

Streaming multimedia allows you to listen to your favorite radio station live on your computer. There are many radio stations around the world that offer streaming multimedia capabilities.

**Rock and Roll Hall of Fame Museum**

www.rrhofm-radio.com

**WMMR 93.3 Philadelphia**

www.wmmr.com

**101.1 TTFM Australia**

www.ttfm.com.au

## CHAPTER 5

# Search the Web

*Do you want to learn how to find information of interest on the Web? In this chapter you will learn how search tools can help you find information quickly and easily.*

# INTRODUCTION TO SEARCHING THE WEB

**There are many ways you can search for information on the Web.**

## SEARCH USING WEB BROWSER

Most new Web browsers allow you to quickly search for information on the Web. Instead of typing a Web page address in the address bar of your Web browser, you may be able to type a question mark (**?**) followed by a word or phrase you want to search for.

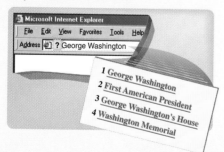

The Web browser will display a list of hyperlinks to Web pages containing the word or phrase you entered. You can click one of the hyperlinks to view the Web page.

## HOW SEARCH TOOLS FIND INFORMATION

There are many Web sites, called search tools, that specialize in helping you search for information. Most search tools have automated robots, called spiders, that travel around the Web looking for new Web pages. People can also submit information about Web pages they have created to search tools.

Since hundreds of new pages are created each day, it is impossible for search tools to catalog every new page on the Web.

## SEARCH TOOL CONSIDERATIONS

### FREE

You do not have to pay to use most search tools to find information on the Web. Most search tools sell advertising space on their Web sites to generate income to pay for the service.

### WEB SITE REVIEWS AND RATINGS

Some search tools have people who review and catalog each new Web page. These people group Web sites containing similar information together in categories to make it easier for you to find the information you want.

When people review Web sites for a search tool, they also examine the quality of information in the Web sites. The search tool may then rate the content of the Web site to help you narrow your search.

### AVAILABLE WEB PAGES

Just as many new pages are created each day, many pages are removed from the Web each day. When you use a search tool to find information on the Web, some of the Web pages you find may have moved or no longer exist. A good search tool checks Web pages frequently to make sure the pages still exist.

# FIND WEB PAGES WITH ALTAVISTA

With over 140 million Web pages in its index, AltaVista is one of the largest search tools on the Web.

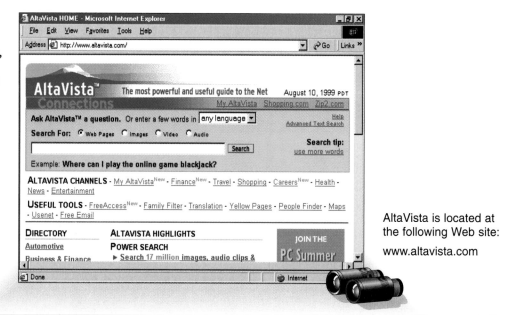

AltaVista is located at the following Web site:

www.altavista.com

## ALTAVISTA SEARCHES

### SEARCH BY WORD OR PHRASE

When performing a search in AltaVista, you type words separated by a space. AltaVista will find Web pages containing one or more of the words you typed. You can search for a specific group of words by typing quotation marks around the group of words you want to find. AltaVista also allows you to enter a complete question to search for Web pages.

### SPECIAL COMMANDS

You can use special commands to make your search more precise. For example, you can type a plus sign (+) in front of a word that must appear on the Web page. You can also type a minus sign (-) in front of a word to indicate you do not want the word to appear on the page.

**ALTAVISTA FEATURES**

## SEARCH FOR SPECIFIC LANGUAGE

You can specify that you want to search for Web pages in a specific language, such as Spanish. When you perform the search, AltaVista will only display links to Web pages in the language you selected.

## SEARCH FOR IMAGES, VIDEOS OR AUDIO FILES

AltaVista maintains collections of images, videos and audio files found on the Web. You can specify that you want to search only a specific collection. For example, you can search the image collection for "solar eclipse" to find pictures of eclipses on the Web.

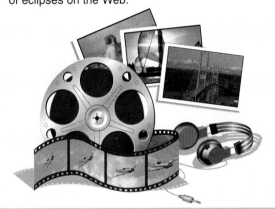

## TRANSLATION

AltaVista offers a translation service. You can have AltaVista translate words, phrases or an entire Web site into a language such as French, German or Italian.

## FAMILY FILTER

AltaVista offers a tool that can help prevent inappropriate or objectionable Web pages from appearing in your search results. You can prevent AltaVista from finding Web pages, images or audio files related to drugs, alcohol, gambling and more.

# FIND WEB PAGES WITH EXCITE

**Excite is a popular search tool that provides an excellent starting point for exploring the Web.**

Excite is located at the following Web site:

www.excite.com

## EXCITE SEARCHES

### SEARCH BY WORD OR PHRASE

You can type a word or phrase into the search area to perform a search using Excite. In addition to finding the words you enter, Excite will also try to find terms related to the words you enter. For example, if you enter "senior citizens," Excite will also find Web pages containing information on "retirement."

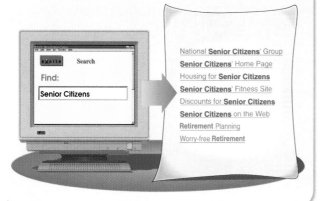

### SEARCH RESULTS

Excite lists your results from most relevant to least relevant. The percentage shown beside each result indicates its relevance.

If one of the results relates closely to the information you want to find, you can select a link to have Excite display similar results.

## EXCITE FEATURES

### BROWSE THROUGH CATEGORIES

You can browse through categories such as autos, careers, health or sports to find information that interests you. When you select a category of interest, a list of subcategories appears. You can continue to select subcategories until you find a Web page that interests you.

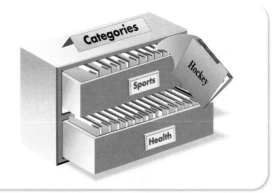

### PERSONALIZED WEB PAGE

Excite allows you to select information that interests you, such as your horoscope, favorite stock quote and local news and weather. Excite will then create a custom Web page for you and will display your customized page each time you visit the Excite Web site. You can even change the colors displayed on the Web page.

### SHORTCUTS TO POPULAR FEATURES

Excite provides you with many shortcuts to the most popular features on the Web. For example, you can quickly access Web sites that allow you to find airline tickets, movie showtimes, maps and much more.

Each day, Excite also displays links to the top news story, a daily poll and other interesting, current features.

# FIND WEB PAGES WITH YAHOO!

Yahoo! is considered one of the best search tools on the Web.

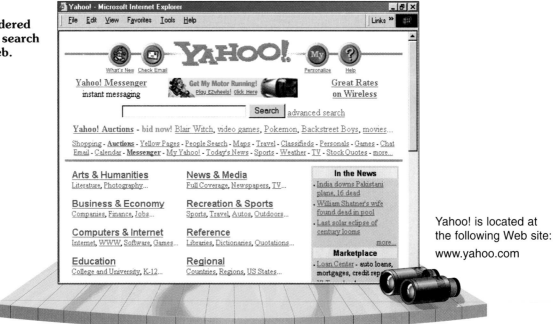

Yahoo! is located at the following Web site:

www.yahoo.com

## CATEGORIES

Every Web site in the Yahoo! directory is reviewed and cataloged by the people at Yahoo!. Web sites containing similar information are grouped together in categories. You can browse through the categories and subcategories until you find Web pages containing the information you want.

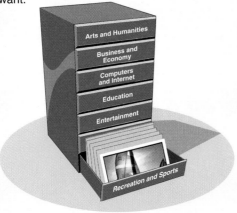

## RATINGS

When people review Web sites for the Yahoo! catalog, they also check out the quality of information in the Web sites. Yahoo! displays a small picture of a pair of sunglasses beside any site that provides good information. When searching Yahoo!, you should try Web sites displaying sunglasses first.

## YAHOO! FEATURES

### NEWS HEADLINES

Yahoo! allows you to read the latest news stories from around the world. Yahoo! gathers the information from various news sources and then displays the information on Web pages. The information is updated approximately once an hour.

### UP-TO-DATE LISTINGS

New Web sites are added to Yahoo! every day. The What's New section lets you quickly find the newest and best Web sites listed at Yahoo!. You can check out the sites listed today or the sites added in the past week.

### PERSONALIZED INFORMATION

You can select topics that interest you, such as sports and entertainment, and have Yahoo! create a custom Web page for you. Your custom Yahoo! page will automatically display only the information you requested. Items such as weather and news stories are updated regularly.

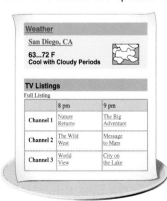

### YAHOOLIGANS!

Yahoo! provides a search tool for children. The search tool offers categories such as social studies, dinosaurs and amusement and theme parks.

# FIND WEB PAGES WITH DOGPILE

**Dogpile sends your search to over 20 different search tools on the Web to help you find the information you are looking for.**

You can find Dogpile at the following Web site:

www.dogpile.com

## DOGPILE SEARCHES

### SEARCH BY WORD

When performing a search using Dogpile, you type words separated by a space. Dogpile will try to find Web pages containing one or more of the words you typed. Dogpile searches three search engines at a time until it finds at least ten Web pages that match the words you typed.

### SPECIAL COMMANDS

You can use special commands to make your search more precise. For example, you can type the word **NOT** in front of a word to indicate you do not want the word to appear on the Web page. You can type the word **NEAR** between two words to indicate that the words must appear near each other on the Web page.

## DOGPILE FEATURES

### STOCK QUOTES

You can use Dogpile to quickly search for stock quotes on the Web. You can specify the name of the company or the ticker symbol for the stock you want to find.

### WEATHER

Dogpile lets you search for the current weather forecast for your city, state or zip code.

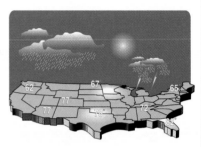

### WEB CATALOG

Dogpile's Web Catalog allows you to browse through categories of information, such as entertainment, health and science, to find Web pages of interest.

### YELLOW PAGES

You can use Dogpile to search the yellow pages for a business you want to find.

### MAPS

You can search for maps of locations in the United States, Canada or other countries around the world. You can specify the address or city you want to display.

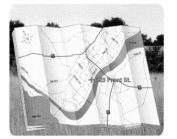

# FIND WEB PAGES WITH SEARCH PROGRAMS

Search programs are programs you run on your own computer. Search programs are useful to people who frequently search the Web for information.

## EFFICIENT

Using a search program is an efficient way to search for information on the Web. Many search programs allow you to perform searches while you complete other tasks. You can also schedule your searches for times that are more convenient, such as during the night.

## COMPREHENSIVE

Search programs often submit information you request to several search tools on the Web. One search tool may offer more information than another search tool but may update Web pages less often. By using a search program, you can search all types of search tools at once.

## SEARCH PROGRAMS

### TELEPORT PRO

Teleport Pro can help you perform in-depth Web searches. You can have Teleport Pro copy an entire Web site to your computer so you can review information without being connected to the Internet.

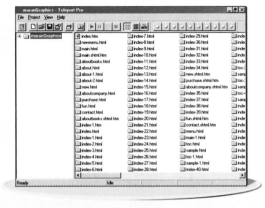

You can also use Teleport Pro to search for files of a specific size and type on the Web. Teleport Pro is available at the following Web site:

www.tenmax.com

### WEBFERRET

WebFerret is one of the fastest search programs available. You can often get results from a search within a few seconds.

You can find WebFerret at the following Web site:

www.ferretsoft.com

### WEBSEEKER 98

WebSeeker 98 allows you to enter a word and then submits the word to more than 100 search tools on the Web. WebSeeker 98 then sorts and displays the results of the search. WebSeeker 98 can also monitor Web pages and inform you when the pages are updated.

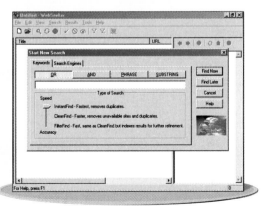

You can find WebSeeker 98 at the following Web site:

www.bluesquirrel.com

# FIND PEOPLE ON THE WEB

You can use the Web to find street addresses, e-mail addresses and telephone numbers for people you want to contact.

## POPULAR SEARCH TOOLS

There are many Web sites that allow you to search for information about people on the Web. You can find some of the most popular search tools at the following Web sites:

people.yahoo.com

www.whowhere.lycos.com

www.555-1212.com

www.infospace.com

## PAID SEARCHES

Some Web sites will help you find information about people for a fee. These Web sites search public records to find information such as property ownership, court records and more. You can find a popular paid search tool at the following Web site:

www.1800ussearch.com

## SEARCH FEATURES

### PROVIDE INFORMATION

You can search for people on the Web by entering a few details about the person you want to find. For example, most search tools require you to enter the first name, last name and city of the person you want to find. The more information you enter, the better the results of the search will be.

### REVERSE SEARCHES

Some search tools allow you to search for information about a person even if you do not know their name. This allows you to find a person by phone number, street address or e-mail address.

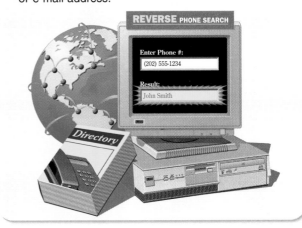

### MAPS

Most search tools allow you to display maps for a street address you enter. You may also be able to display driving directions between your address and the address of the person you found.

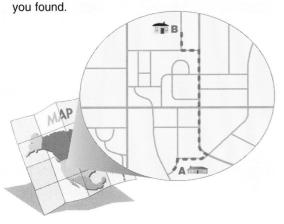

### GOVERNMENT LISTINGS

Some Web sites include a directory of United States government officials. You can find information on federal and state governments as well as various committees. You can use the directory to find out how to contact the government officials for your area.

## CHAPTER 6

# Create Web Pages

*Do you want to learn more about creating and publishing your own Web pages? This chapter introduces you to the basics of Web publishing.*

# REASONS FOR CREATING WEB PAGES

**Creating and publishing your own Web pages allows millions of people around the world to view your information.**

PERSONAL

## SHARE PERSONAL INFORMATION

Many people create Web pages to share information about their families, pets, vacations or favorite hobbies. Some people create Web pages to present a résumé to potential employers.

## SHARE KNOWLEDGE

Many scientists and business professionals make their work available on the Web. If you are experienced in an area that many people are unfamiliar with, you can create Web pages to share your knowledge.

## ENTERTAIN VISITORS

Many people create Web pages to display collections of jokes or humorous stories. You can also create Web pages to display information, pictures, sound clips and videos about a favorite celebrity, sports team or TV show.

## PROMOTE INTERESTS

You can create Web pages to display information about an organization or club that you belong to. You can include a schedule of upcoming events and detailed information about the goals of the organization.

## COMMERCIAL

### PROVIDE INFORMATION

Companies often place pages on the Web to provide information about their company and the products and services they offer. Companies can use Web pages to keep the public informed about new products and interesting news. Many companies display their press releases on the Web.

### SHOPPING

Many companies create Web pages that allow readers to order products and services over the Internet. Companies can display descriptions and pictures of products to help readers determine which products they want to purchase.

### JOB LISTINGS

Many companies use Web pages to advertise jobs that are available within the company. Some companies allow readers to submit résumés through their Web site.

### CONTACT INFORMATION

Companies can display their office addresses and phone numbers on their Web pages. This helps readers contact the company to ask questions and express opinions.

# STEPS FOR CREATING WEB PAGES

There are several steps you should follow to create and publish Web pages.

World Wide Web

For an in-depth look at creating Web pages, check out maranGraphics' **Creating Web Pages with HTML Simplified, 2nd Edition**, published by IDG Books Worldwide, Inc.

## 1 PLAN YOUR WEB PAGES

Decide what you want to accomplish with your Web pages. Decide on a main topic or theme for your Web pages and then determine the type of information you want to include.

WEB PAGE

## 2 GATHER INFORMATION

Collect the information you want to include on your Web pages, such as text, pictures, diagrams and contact numbers. Make sure the information you gather directly relates to the main topic or theme you chose for your Web pages.

The Fishing Guide

## 3 ORGANIZE INFORMATION

Divide the information you gathered into sections. Each section should be a separate Web page. Each Web page should discuss a different concept or idea and should contain enough information to fill a single screen.

Introduction to Fishing

Fishing Pictures

Links to Fishing Pages

**ENTER TEXT**

Enter the text you want to appear on your Web pages in a text editor or word processor. Each Web page should be a separate document. You can then convert the documents into Web pages.

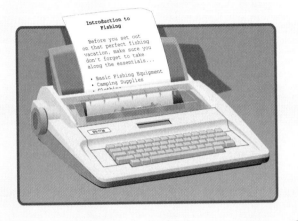

**ADD IMAGES**

You can add images to enhance the appearance of your Web pages. You can create your own images and obtain images at computer stores or on the Internet. For more information on images, see page 120.

**ADD HYPERLINKS**

You can add hyperlinks that readers can select on your Web pages to display other pages on the Web. Hyperlinks allow readers to easily move through information of interest. For more information on hyperlinks, see page 118.

**PUBLISH WEB PAGES**

When you finish creating your Web pages, you can transfer the pages to a computer that makes pages available on the Web. You should then test the Web pages to ensure your hyperlinks work properly and your information appears the way you want.

# PROGRAMS FOR CREATING WEB PAGES

You can choose between several types of programs to create Web pages.

Web pages are HTML documents, which consist of text and special instructions, called tags. Each tag gives a specific instruction and is surrounded by angle brackets < >.

HTML documents have the .html or .htm extension (example: index.html).

## TEXT EDITOR OR WORD PROCESSOR

### Text Editor

A text editor is a simple program you can use to create and edit documents that contain only text. Popular text editors include Notepad for Windows and SimpleText for Macintosh.

### Word Processor

A word processor is a program that provides advanced editing and formatting features to help you create documents. Any formatting you apply to text will not appear when you view documents you create on the Web. Popular word processors include Microsoft Word and Corel WordPerfect.

To create a Web page using a text editor or word processor, you must type the text for the Web page and then add HTML tags to specify how you want the text to appear on the Web page. You need a Web browser to see how the Web page will appear on the Web.

## HTML EDITOR

An HTML editor is a program you can use to create Web pages. HTML editors offer menus and toolbars that you can use to add HTML tags to your Web pages. Many HTML editors include a validator that can check your Web pages for HTML errors. You need to know HTML to create a Web page using an HTML editor.

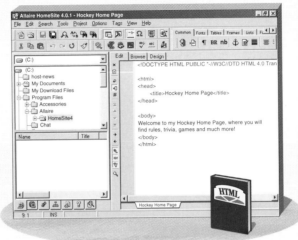

Some HTML editors allow you to see how Web pages you create will appear on the Web, while others require you to use a Web browser to view your Web pages.

You can obtain HTML editors at the following Web sites:

**BBEdit**
www.barebones.com

**HomeSite**
www.allaire.com

## VISUAL EDITOR

A visual editor is a program you can use to graphically create Web pages. Visual editors make it easier to create Web pages because they enter the HTML tags for you. You do not need to know HTML to create a Web page using a visual editor.

Visual editors allow you to instantly see how a change you make will affect the Web page.

You can obtain visual editors at the following Web sites:

**HoTMetaL PRO**
www.softquad.com

**Microsoft FrontPage**
www.microsoft.com/frontpage

# THE HOME PAGE

The home page is the main Web page in a Web site. The home page is usually the first page people see when they visit a Web site.

The home page is usually named **index.html** or **index.htm**. You should check with the company that makes your pages available on the Web to determine what name to use.

## SUMMARY

Always include a brief summary of your Web pages on the home page. You should state whether the purpose of your Web pages is to entertain or inform readers. You should not assume that readers will understand the purpose of your Web pages just by reading the title.

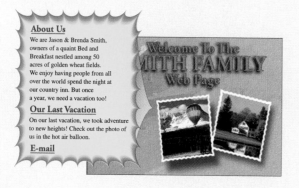

## TABLE OF CONTENTS

Your home page should include a table of contents that lists the information in your Web site. You should include hyperlinks that allow readers to quickly access information of interest.

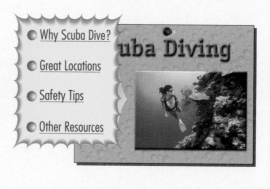

## BOOKMARK REMINDER

Web browsers have a feature, called bookmarks or favorites, that allows readers to store the addresses of Web pages they visit. You can include an image or phrase on your home page to remind readers to bookmark your Web page. This allows readers to quickly return to your Web site.

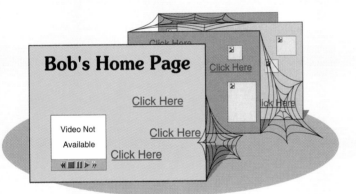

## MAKE A GOOD IMPRESSION

Your home page should include interesting, well-organized information. You should also make sure any links or multimedia you added to the home page work properly. If readers find your home page disorganized or difficult to use, they may not view the other pages in your Web site.

## ENHANCEMENTS

You can add many types of enhancements to help add interest to your home page. You can add items such as a hit counter that records the number of visitors to your home page, a clock that displays the current time in your city or a guest book where visitors can record their comments.

# WEB PAGE CONTENT CONSIDERATIONS

When creating Web pages, you should carefully consider the content of the pages.

## EXAMINE YOUR FAVORITE WEB PAGES

Before you start creating Web pages, examine some of your favorite Web pages. Determine what you like about the Web pages and consider how you can use these ideas on your pages.

## PROOFREAD INFORMATION

Carefully check your Web pages for spelling and grammar errors. Spelling mistakes will make readers think that you are careless and that your Web pages are inaccurate. You may want to print your Web pages to help you proofread the pages.

## EMPHASIZE IMPORTANT INFORMATION

If some parts of your Web page are more important than others, use the available formatting features to make the information stand out. Do not bury important ideas or concepts in long paragraphs.

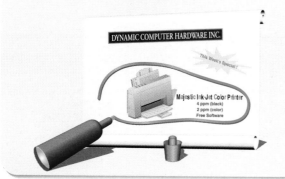

## AVOID "UNDER CONSTRUCTION" LABELS

You should avoid using "under construction" labels for Web pages that are not complete. You will frustrate readers when they visit a Web page that does not contain useful information. Do not make a page available on the Web until the page is complete.

## UPDATE INFORMATION

You should update your Web pages on a regular basis. If the information on your Web pages never changes, people will only read the pages once and will not revisit them in the future. You should include the date on your Web pages to let readers know when you last updated the pages.

## INCLUDE CONTACT INFORMATION

Always include your name and e-mail address on Web pages you create. This allows readers to contact you if they have questions or comments.

## CONSIDER WEB PAGES WITHOUT IMAGES

Some people turn off the display of images to browse the Web more quickly, while other people use Web browsers that cannot display images. Always design your Web pages so that readers who do not see images will still get valuable information from your pages.

## CONSIDER TRANSFER SPEED

When creating your Web pages, try to keep the file size of the pages and images as small as possible. This will speed up the display of your Web pages by reducing the time it takes for the information to transfer.

# HYPERLINKS

You can link text or an image on your Web page to another page in your Web site or to any page on the Web.

When viewing your Web pages, readers can immediately view a related page by selecting a hyperlink. Hyperlinks are also referred to as links.

## CREATE DESCRIPTIVE LINKS

Make sure the text or image you use to create a hyperlink clearly indicates where the link will take the reader. Do not use the phrase "Click Here" for a hyperlink, since this phrase is not very descriptive and forces readers to examine the surrounding text to determine where the link will take them.

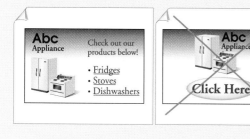

## INCLUDE TEXT LINKS

If your Web page contains image links, you should also provide corresponding text links for your readers. Some readers turn off the display of images to browse more quickly, while others use Web browsers that cannot display images.

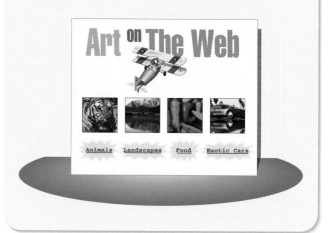

## REASONS FOR HYPERLINKS

### NAVIGATIONAL LINKS

You should include navigational links to help readers move through your Web pages. Navigational links can include hyperlinks to a table of contents or to your home page.

### LINKS TO LARGE IMAGES

You can create a hyperlink that will take readers to a large image. For example, you can link a small version of an image, called a thumbnail image, to a larger version of the image. This lets readers decide if they want to wait to view the larger image.

### DEFINITION LINKS

If your Web page contains technical terms your readers may not understand, you should consider including definition links that will take readers to a footnote or brief explanation.

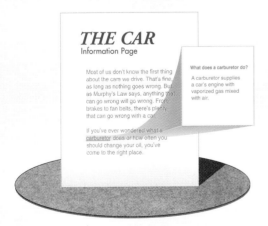

### E-MAIL LINKS

You can create a hyperlink that allows readers to quickly send you an e-mail message. This is a great way to gather comments about your Web pages. Many companies display e-mail links for each person in the company on a Web page. This helps readers contact the appropriate person.

# IMAGES

You can add an image to a Web page. An image that appears on a Web page is called an inline image.

## GET IMAGES

Many Web sites offer images that you can use for free on your Web pages. You can use a scanner to scan images into your computer or create your own images. You can also buy a collection of ready-made images at a computer store. Make sure you have permission to use any images you did not create yourself.

## IMAGE TYPES

When adding images to your Web pages, you should use GIF or JPEG images. These are the most popular types of images on the Web.

GIF (Graphics Interchange Format) images are limited to 256 colors and are often used for logos, banners and computer-generated art. GIF images have the .gif extension (example: logo.gif).

JPEG (Joint Photographic Experts Group) images can have millions of colors and are often used for photographs and very large images. JPEG images usually have the .jpg extension (example: racecar.jpg).

## WAYS TO USE IMAGES

### ART AND PHOTOGRAPHS

A Web page can display drawings, paintings or computer-generated art. Graphic artists and design companies often display art on their Web pages to advertise their work. You can also display photographs of your family, pets or favorite celebrities on your Web pages.

### EXPLANATIONS

An image can help clarify a concept that is difficult to explain with words. You can include a map to give directions, a chart to show financial trends or a diagram to point out parts of a product.

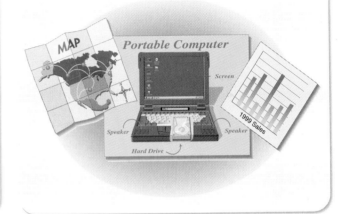

### BACKGROUND IMAGES

You can have a small image repeat to fill an entire Web page. This can add an interesting background design to your Web page. You should make sure the background image you choose does not affect the readability of your Web page.

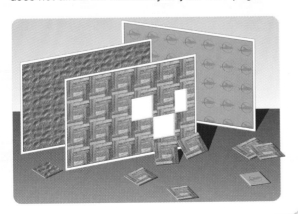

### IMAGE MAPS

You can divide an image into different areas and link each area to a different Web page. This is called an image map. When creating an image map, you should use an image that has several distinct areas that readers can select.

# STYLE SHEETS

You can use style sheets to define the formatting and layout of your Web pages.

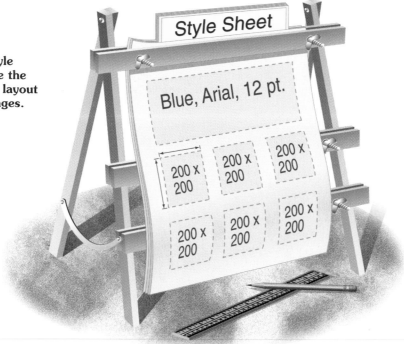

Style sheets are also known as Cascading Style Sheets (CSS).

Some older Web browsers cannot understand style sheets.

## REASONS FOR USING STYLE SHEETS

### ADDITIONAL FEATURES

Style sheets allow you to format text and lay out Web pages in ways you cannot accomplish using HTML tags. You can create sophisticated Web pages that look like pages from a magazine.

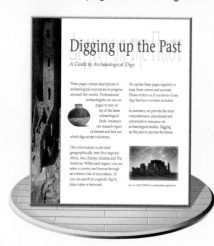

### SAVE TIME

Style sheets allow you to specify in one centralized location how you want information to appear on a Web page. For example, you can specify that you want all of your main headings to appear in a specific font and color. Any changes you make using style sheets will affect the entire Web page.

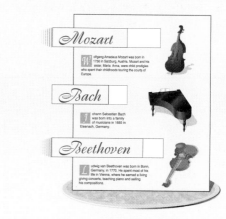

**Before publishing your Web pages, you must prepare to transfer the pages to a Web server.**

## CHECK WEB PAGE FILE NAMES

Your Web page file names should all have the .htm or .html extension (example: garden.html) and should not include spaces or special characters, such as * or &.

## ORGANIZE WEB PAGE FILES

You should place all of your Web pages in one folder. Make sure the folder also contains all the images, sounds, videos and other files included on your Web pages. If the folder contains many files, you may want to place some of the files in subfolders.

For example, you can store all of your images in a subfolder. If you change the location of any files, make sure you update all references to the files on your Web pages.

## OBTAIN AN FTP PROGRAM

You need a File Transfer Protocol (FTP) program to transfer your Web pages to a Web server. You can find two of the most popular FTP programs at the following Web sites:

**WS_FTP Pro (Windows)**

www.ipswitch.com/products

**Fetch (Macintosh)**

www.macorchard.com/ftp.html

# WEB PRESENCE PROVIDERS

Web presence providers are companies that store Web pages and make them available on the Web. Web presence providers store Web pages on computers called Web servers.

## INTERNET ACCESS PROVIDERS

Internet access providers usually offer space on their Web servers where their customers can publish Web pages free of charge.

## FREE WEB PRESENCE PROVIDERS

There are many companies on the Web that will publish your Web pages for free. These companies offer a limited amount of storage space and may place advertisements on your Web pages.

You can find companies that will publish your Web pages for free at the following Web sites:

www.geocities.com

www.tripod.com

## DEDICATED WEB PRESENCE PROVIDERS

Dedicated Web presence providers are companies that specialize in publishing Web pages for a fee. These companies offer features that other Web presence providers do not offer.

You can find dedicated Web presence providers at the following Web sites:

www.dreamhost.com

www.hostess.com

www.pair.com

## WEB PRESENCE PROVIDER CONSIDERATIONS

### TECHNICAL SUPPORT

A Web presence provider should have a technical support department to answer your questions. You should be able to contact the department by telephone or e-mail.

### STORAGE SPACE

Most Web presence providers limit the amount of space you can use to store your Web pages. Choose a Web presence provider that allows you to store at least 5 MB (megabytes) of information.

### DOMAIN NAME REGISTRATION

For a fee, most Web presence providers allow you to choose the address, or domain name, that people type to access your Web pages. A personalized domain name is easy for people to remember and will not change if you switch to another Web presence provider.

### ACCESS LOGS

A good Web presence provider will supply you with statistics about your Web pages, such as which of your Web pages are the most popular and where your visitors are from. Access logs can help you determine if you need to make changes to your Web pages.

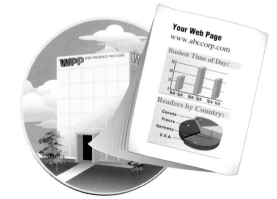

# TEST YOUR WEB PAGES

**You should test your Web pages to make sure they look and work the way you planned.**

Test your Web pages to see how easily you can browse through the information. Make sure your Web pages have a consistent design and writing style and do not contain formatting or layout errors.

## VIEW IN DIFFERENT WEB BROWSERS

You should view your Web pages in different Web browsers to make sure the pages look the way you planned. Each Web browser will display your Web pages in a slightly different way. Test your Web pages with the two most popular Web browsers–Microsoft Internet Explorer and Netscape Navigator.

**Microsoft Internet Explorer**          **Netscape Navigator**

## VIEW AT DIFFERENT RESOLUTIONS

The resolution of a monitor determines the amount of information that will appear on a screen. Readers will view your Web pages at different resolutions. You should view your Web pages at the two most popular resolutions–640x480 and 800x600.

**640x480**          **800x600**

## VIEW ON DIFFERENT COMPUTERS

Web pages can look different when displayed on different computers. You should view your Web pages on different computers to ensure the pages appear the way you planned.

## CHECK LINKS

You should regularly check the links on your Web pages to make sure they will take your readers to the intended destinations. Make sure the linked Web pages still exist and contain useful information.

## TURN OFF IMAGES

Some people turn off the display of images to browse the Web more quickly, while others use Web browsers that cannot display images. You should view your Web pages without images to ensure that readers who do not see images will still find your pages useful.

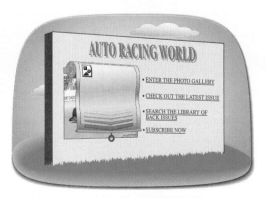

## TRANSFER SPEED

Determine how long your Web pages take to appear at different transfer speeds. Many people use modems that transfer information at 56 Kbps, but slower modems are still common. Web pages with large file sizes may take a long time to transfer.

# PUBLICIZE YOUR WEB PAGES

After you publish your Web pages, there are several ways you can let people know about the pages.

## E-MAIL MESSAGES

Most e-mail programs have a feature that allows you to add information, called a signature, to the end of every e-mail message you send. You can include information about your Web pages in your signature.

## EXCHANGE LINKS

If another page on the Web discusses ideas related to your Web pages, you can ask if the author of the page will include a link to your pages if you do the same. This lets people reading the other Web page easily visit your Web pages.

## WEB PAGE ADVERTISEMENTS

Many companies set aside areas on their Web pages where you can advertise your Web pages. The LinkExchange helps you advertise your Web pages free of charge. The LinkExchange is located at the **adnetwork.linkexchange.com** Web site.

## NEWSGROUPS

You can send an announcement about your Web pages to newsgroups. Make sure you choose newsgroups that discuss topics related to your Web pages. You can announce new or updated Web pages on the **comp.infosystems.www.announce** newsgroup.

## MAILING LISTS

You can send an announcement to carefully selected mailing lists. You should read the messages in a mailing list for a week before sending an announcement to make sure the mailing list members would be interested in your Web pages.

## SEARCH TOOLS

You can submit your Web pages to various search tools on the Web so people can easily find your Web pages. You can view descriptions of the top 100 search tools at the **www.mmgco.com/top100.html** Web site. You can submit your Web pages to many search tools at once at the **www.submit-it.com** Web site.

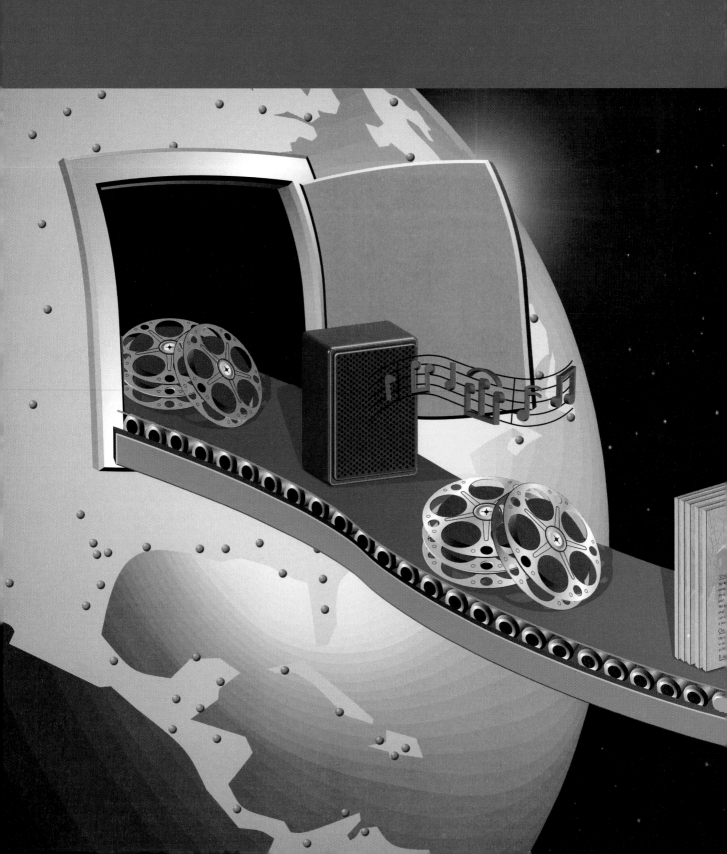

## CHAPTER 7

# Download Information from the Internet

*Are you wondering how to download files and programs from the Internet? Learn how in this chapter.*

# DOWNLOAD ITEMS FROM WEB PAGES

You can download, or save, items of interest from a page on the Web. You can download a displayed image, download an entire Web page or use a hyperlink to download a file.

After you download an item to your computer, you can access the item at any time.

## DOWNLOAD A DISPLAYED IMAGE

Most Web browsers allow you to download an image displayed on a Web page to your computer. After the image is saved on your computer, you can use the image in your own documents. Make sure you have permission to use any image you download from the Web.

## DOWNLOAD A WEB PAGE

Most Web browsers allow you to download an entire Web page on your computer. This allows you to view the Web page when you are not connected to the Internet or send the Web page to a friend or colleague using an e-mail program.

Web pages often provide hyperlinks you can use to download files. There are many different types of files you can download.

## DOWNLOAD A FILE USING A HYPERLINK

### DOWNLOAD TEXT FILES

You can get interesting documents for research and enjoyment. You can obtain books, computer manuals, government documents, news summaries and academic papers.

### DOWNLOAD IMAGE FILES

You can download images, such as computer-generated art, museum paintings and pictures of famous people. Popular image formats on the Web include Bitmap, GIF, JPEG and PNG.

### DOWNLOAD SOUND FILES

You can download theme songs, sound effects, clips of famous speeches and lines from television shows and movies. Popular sound formats include MIDI, MPEG, RealAudio and Wave.

### DOWNLOAD VIDEO FILES

You can download movie clips, cartoons, educational videos and computer-generated animation. Popular video formats on the Web include AVI, MPEG and QuickTime.

# DOWNLOAD PROGRAMS

You can download programs from the Web to use on your computer, such as word processors, spreadsheets, e-mail programs, screen savers, games and much more.

Software companies, such as Microsoft and Netscape, usually allow you to download programs from their Web sites. There are also many Web sites that allow you to search through huge collections of programs for downloading. The following Web sites provide a wide variety of programs you can download to your computer:

www.shareware.com

www.tucows.com

www.jumbo.com

## PROGRAM DESCRIPTIONS

Most Web sites provide a short description of each program you can download, including the size of the program and the system requirements you need to run the program. Many Web sites also provide reviews of the program, written by people who have used the program.

## TYPES OF PROGRAMS

### FREEWARE

Freeware programs are free but have copyright restrictions. The author may require you to follow certain rules if you want to change or distribute freeware programs.

**Free!
(with restrictions)**

◆ You must include the author's name (and this file) wherever the program is distributed.

◆ You must not sell this program.

◆ You must not change program in any way.

◆ You must fill in and registration form.

Freeware Program

### SHAREWARE

You can try a shareware program free of charge for a limited time. If you like the program and want to continue using it, you must pay the author of the program. Shareware programs often do not let you use all the features of the program until you pay for the program.

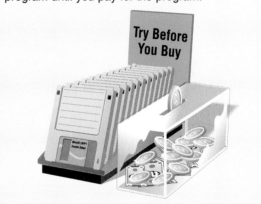

Try Before
You Buy

### BETA VERSION

A beta version of a program is an early version of the program that is not quite ready for release. Many software companies let people use and test the beta version of a program for free before releasing the official version.

Web Browser

Beta Version

### TRIAL VERSION

You can download a trial version of a program. Trial versions usually allow you to use all of the features of a program for a limited time. After the trial period, you must purchase the program if you want to continue using the program.

IMAGEPAINTER
Cannot open program.
Your trial period has expired!

OK

IMAGEPAINTER

TRIAL VERSION

# DOWNLOAD MP3 MUSIC

You can download, or copy, CD-quality music to your computer from the Web.

Your computer must have sound capabilities to play CD-quality music.

MP3 is a sound format used to transfer CD-quality music over the Internet. MP3 stands for Motion Picture Experts Group Audio Layer 3. The MP3 format compresses sound files so they take up small amounts of disk space. The small size of MP3 files allows the files to transfer quickly and easily over the Internet.

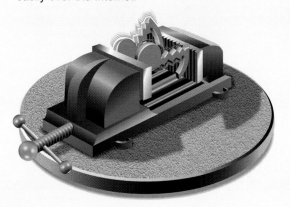

**USING MP3**

Recording artists distribute their music in MP3 format on the Web to promote their music. There are many Web sites that allow you to download individual songs or entire CDs in MP3 format to your computer. Some sites offer the music for free and some require you to purchase the music. You can find MP3 files at the following Web sites:

www.emusic.com

www.mp3.com

www.mp3place.com

## MP3 PLAYER

You need special software, called an MP3 player, installed on your computer to download and play MP3 files. Most MP3 players on the Web are free or offer a free trial version.

Some MP3 players look and act like a CD player. They have play, pause and stop buttons as well as balance, volume and equalizer controls. You can find MP3 players at the following Web sites:

**Winamp (Windows)**

www.winamp.com

**MacAMP (Macintosh)**

www.macamp.org

**Media Player (Windows and Macintosh)**

www.microsoft.com/windows/mediaplayer

## PORTABLE MP3 PLAYER

You can use a portable MP3 player to listen to your MP3 files. After you download songs from the Web, you can transfer the songs from your computer to the portable player and take them with you. Most portable MP3 players can hold up to an hour's worth of CD-quality music. You can find portable MP3 players at many electronics stores.

Most portable MP3 players are solid-state devices, which means they have no moving parts. This allows you to listen to music while you are jogging or exercising without worrying about the music skipping.

# DOWNLOAD FILES USING FTP

FTP (File Transfer Protocol) lets you look through files stored on computers around the world and download, or copy, files that interest you.

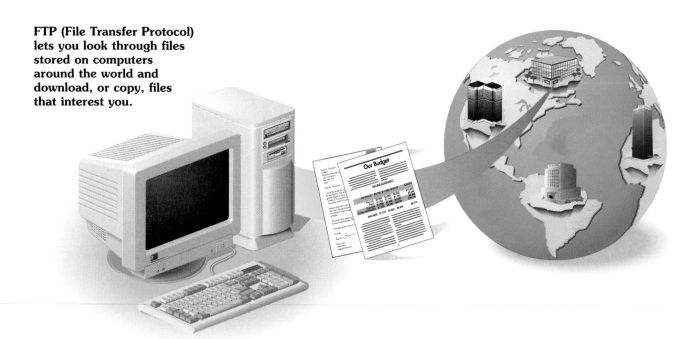

## FTP SITES

An FTP site stores files that people can download free of charge. Some FTP sites require you to enter a password before you can access any files. Colleges, universities, government agencies, companies and individuals maintain FTP sites. You can find a list of FTP sites at the following Web site:

hoohoo.ncsa.uiuc.edu/ftp-interface.html

## DOWNLOAD FILES

Many people use their Web browser to download files from an FTP site. You can also use an FTP program to download files. Using an FTP program is useful if you want to download several files to your computer at once. You can find two of the most popular FTP programs at the following Web sites:

**WS_FTP Pro (Windows)**

www.ipswitch.com/products

**Fetch (Macintosh)**

www.macorchard.com/ftp.html

## HOW FILES ARE STORED AT FTP SITES

### DIRECTORIES

Files at FTP sites are stored in different directories. Directories organize information at an FTP site, just as folders organize documents in a filing cabinet.

Most FTP sites have a main directory called "pub," which is short for public. The pub directory contains subdirectories and files. Most subdirectory names indicate what type of files the subdirectory contains. Common subdirectory names include "apps" for software applications and "docs" for text files and documents.

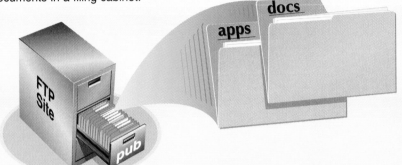

### FILE NAMES

Every file stored at an FTP site has a **name** and an **extension**, separated by a period (.). The name describes the contents of a file. The extension usually identifies the type of file.

### README FILES

Most well established FTP sites include files that describe the rest of the files offered at the site. These files are usually named "readme" or "index" and are usually found in the main directory at an FTP site.

# DOWNLOAD CONSIDERATIONS

**There are several factors to consider when you download files from the Internet.**

## FILE COMPRESSION

Many large files stored on the Internet are compressed, or squeezed, to make them smaller. Compressed files transfer more quickly over the Internet.

After you transfer a compressed file to your computer, you may need to use a compression program to expand the file before you can use the file. You can find compression programs at the following Web sites:

**WinZip (Windows)**       **StuffIt (Macintosh)**

www.winzip.com       www.aladdinsys.com/products

## COMPATIBILITY

Just because you can transfer a file to your computer does not mean you can use the file. Make sure you get files that can work with your type of computer. Many sites on the Internet have separate areas for Macintosh and IBM-compatible computers.

When you download a file, you must also ensure that you have a program installed that can play or display the file.

### BUSY WEB SITES

Each Web site can let only a certain number of people use the site at once. If you get an error message when you try to connect, the site may already have as many people connected as it can handle. Try accessing the Web site again outside business hours, such as at night or on the weekend.

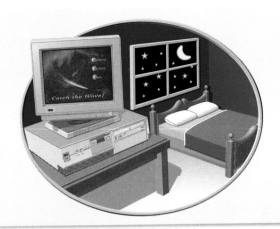

### MIRROR SITES

Some popular Web sites have mirror sites. A mirror site stores exactly the same information as the original site but is usually less busy. A mirror site may also be geographically closer to your computer, which can provide a faster and more reliable connection.

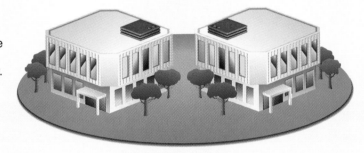

Mirror sites are updated regularly to ensure the files available at the original site are also available at the mirror site.

### VIRUSES

A virus is a destructive computer program that can disrupt the normal operation of a computer. You should use an anti-virus program to check for viruses on files you download from the Internet.

You can find popular anti-virus tools at the following Web sites:

www.mcafee.com

www.symantec.com/nav/index.html

housecall.antivirus.com

## CHAPTER 8

# Electronic Mail

*Would you like to communicate with family, friends and colleagues on the Internet? Read this chapter to find out how to use electronic mail.*

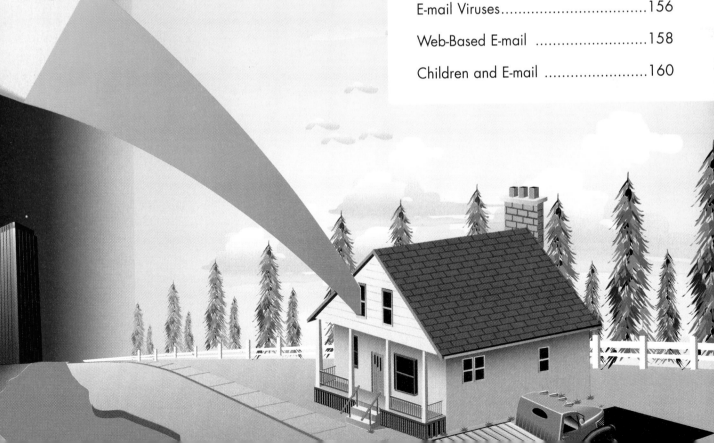

# INTRODUCTION TO E-MAIL

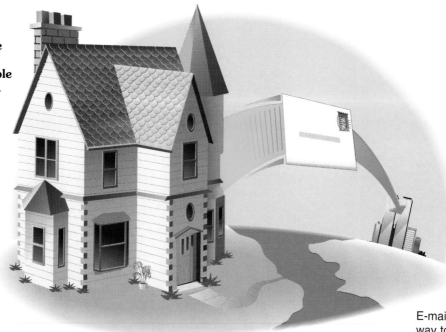

You can exchange electronic mail (e-mail) with people around the world.

E-mail is a convenient way to send messages to family, friends and colleagues.

## SPEED

E-mail is much faster than old-fashioned mail, called "snail mail." An e-mail message can travel around the world in minutes.

## COST

Once you pay a service provider for a connection to the Internet, there is no charge for sending and receiving e-mail. You do not have to pay extra even if you send a long message or the message travels around the world.

Exchanging e-mail can save you money on long distance calls. The next time you are about to pick up the telephone, consider sending an e-mail message instead.

## CONVENIENCE

You can create and send e-mail messages at any time. Unlike telephone calls, e-mail messages do not require the person receiving the message to be at their computer when you send the message. E-mail makes communicating with people in different time zones very convenient.

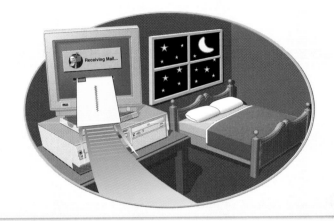

## COMPOSE OFFLINE

You can write e-mail messages when you are not connected to the Internet. This is called working offline. When you finish writing all your messages, you can connect to the Internet and send the messages all at once. This can save you money since you do not have to pay for the time you spend composing messages.

## HEADERS

Every e-mail message contains information called a header. You can view the header to find information such as the date and time the message was sent. You can also view a list of all the computers on the Internet the message passed through before reaching your computer.

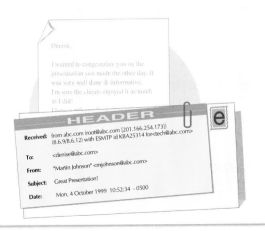

# E-MAIL PROGRAMS

An e-mail program lets you send, receive and manage your e-mail messages.

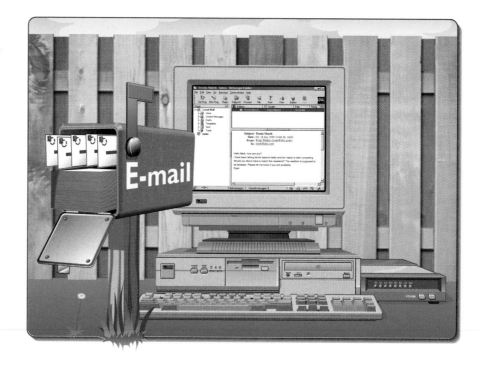

Popular e-mail programs include Eudora Light and Netscape Mail.

**Eudora Light**

eudora.qualcomm.com

**Netscape Mail**

www.netscape.com

*Note: Netscape Mail is part of the Netscape Communicator suite.*

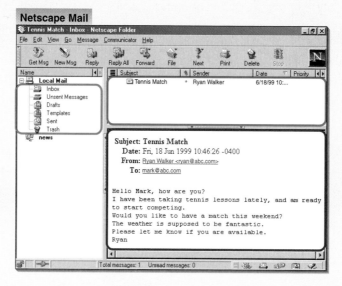

■ This area displays the folders that contain your e-mail messages.

■ This area displays a list of all your e-mail messages.

■ This area displays the contents of a single e-mail message.

## E-MAIL PROGRAM FEATURES

### ORGANIZATION

E-mail programs usually store messages you have sent, received and deleted in separate folders. This helps you keep messages organized so you can review them later. You can also create personalized folders to better organize your messages.

### FILTERS

Some e-mail programs can automatically sort your e-mail messages into folders for you. This is called filtering. You can create a simple filter to have the e-mail program place all messages from a certain person in one folder.

### SPELL CHECKING

Most e-mail programs include a spell check feature. Before you send a message, the spell checker compares every word in the message to words in its dictionary. If a word does not exist in the dictionary, the spell checker considers the word misspelled. The spell checker will ask if you want to change the spelling of the word and may suggest a replacement.

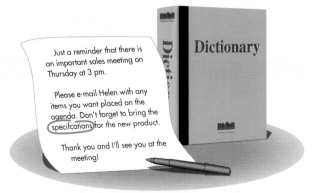

# E-MAIL ADDRESSES

**You can send a message to anyone around the world if you know the person's e-mail address.**

An e-mail address defines the location of an individual's mailbox on the Internet.

An e-mail address consists of two parts separated by the @ ("at") symbol. An e-mail address cannot contain spaces.

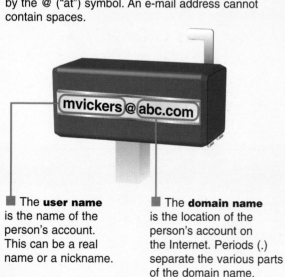

■ The **user name** is the name of the person's account. This can be a real name or a nickname.

■ The **domain name** is the location of the person's account on the Internet. Periods (.) separate the various parts of the domain name.

### FAMOUS E-MAIL ADDRESSES

| NAME | ADDRESS |
|---|---|
| Bill Gates | askbill@microsoft.com |
| Brad Pitt | ciaobox@msn.com |
| Madonna | madonna@wbr.com |
| U.S. President | president@whitehouse.gov |
| Tom Brokaw | nightly@nbc.com |

## ORGANIZATION OR COUNTRY

The last few characters in an e-mail address usually indicate the type of organization or country to which the person belongs.

### ORGANIZATION

| | |
|---|---|
| com | commercial |
| edu | education |
| gov | government |
| mil | military |
| net | network |
| org | organization (often non-profit) |

### COUNTRY

| | |
|---|---|
| au | Australia |
| ca | Canada |
| it | Italy |
| jp | Japan |
| uk | United Kingdom |

PASSPORT

## FIND E-MAIL ADDRESSES

The best way to find the e-mail addresses of friends or colleagues is to phone them and ask. Although there is no central listing of e-mail addresses, there are many places on the Web that help you search for e-mail addresses.

You can search for e-mail addresses at the following Web sites:

people.yahoo.com

www.bigfoot.com

# PARTS OF A MESSAGE

**From:**

Address of the person sending the message.

**To:**

Address of the person receiving the message.

| From: | mary@abc.com |
|---|---|
| To: | john@abc.com |
| Subject: | Sales Awards |
| Cc: | sarah@abc.com |
| Bcc: | karen@abc.com |

Congratulations on your achievement! I'm looking forward to seeing you at the Awards Ceremony!

**Subject:**

Identifies the contents of the message. Make sure your subject is informative. Do not use subjects such as "For your information" or "Read this now."

**Cc:**

Stands for "carbon copy." A carbon copy is an exact copy of a message. You can send a carbon copy of a message to a person who is not directly involved, but would be interested in the message.

**Bcc:**

Stands for "blind carbon copy." Sending a blind carbon copy of a message lets you send an exact copy of the message to a person without the other recipients knowing that the person received the message.

## RECEIVE MESSAGES

Your computer does not have to be turned on for you to receive e-mail messages. Your Internet access provider stores the messages you receive in a mailbox. When you check for new messages, you are checking your mailbox on the access provider's computer.

You should check for new messages on a regular basis. If your mailbox gets too full, your access provider may delete some of your messages.

You can use most computers on the Internet to connect to your access provider and retrieve your messages. This allows you to check your messages while traveling.

## AUTOMATICALLY CHECK FOR MESSAGES

Most e-mail programs automatically check for new e-mail messages. You can specify how often you want the program to check for new messages.

You should have the e-mail program check for messages approximately every 30 minutes. If your e-mail program is constantly checking for new messages, it can slow down the performance of other tasks, such as browsing the Web.

# SEND A MESSAGE

**You can send a message to exchange ideas or request information.**

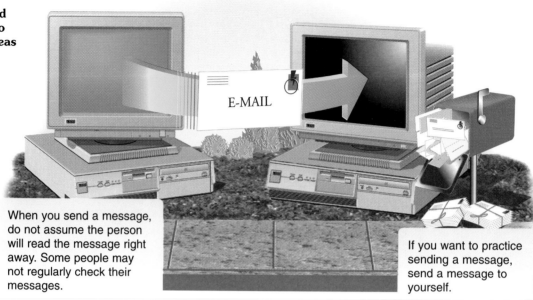

When you send a message, do not assume the person will read the message right away. Some people may not regularly check their messages.

If you want to practice sending a message, send a message to yourself.

## ADDRESS BOOK

Most e-mail programs provide an address book where you can store the addresses of people you frequently send messages to. An address book saves you from having to type the same addresses over and over again.

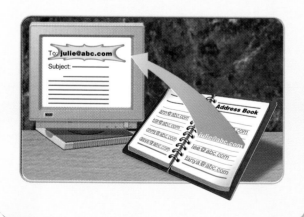

## WRITING STYLE

Make sure every message you send is clear, concise and contains no spelling or grammar errors. Also make sure your message will not be misinterpreted. For example, the reader may not realize a statement is meant to be sarcastic.

## SMILEYS

You can use special characters, called smileys or emoticons, to express emotions in messages. These characters resemble human faces if you turn them sideways.

## ABBREVIATIONS

Abbreviations are commonly used in messages to save time typing.

| Abbreviation | Meaning | Abbreviation | Meaning |
|---|---|---|---|
| BTW | by the way | LOL | laughing out loud |
| FAQ | frequently asked questions | MOTAS | member of the appropriate sex |
| FOAF | friend of a friend | MOTOS | member of the opposite sex |
| FWIW | for what it's worth | | |
| FYI | for your information | MOTSS | member of the same sex |
| IMHO | in my humble opinion | | |
| | | ROTFL | rolling on the floor laughing |
| IMO | in my opinion | | |
| IOW | in other words | SO | significant other |
| L8R | later | WRT | with respect to |

## SHOUTING

A MESSAGE WRITTEN IN CAPITAL LETTERS IS ANNOYING AND HARD TO READ. THIS IS CALLED SHOUTING. Always use upper and lower case letters when typing messages.

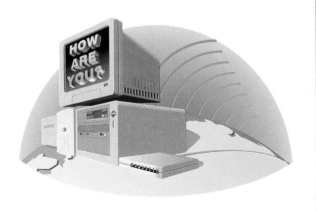

## SIGNATURE

You can have an e-mail program add information about yourself to the end of every message you send. This prevents you from having to type the same information over and over again.

A signature can include your name, e-mail address, occupation or favorite quotation.

## SEND A MESSAGE TO MANY ADDRESSES

You can send a message to many e-mail addresses at once. To do so, you must first assign a name to a group of e-mail addresses. When you send a message to the name you assigned to the group, the message will be sent to every e-mail address in the group. This feature is useful if you want to send announcements or newsletters to everyone on a mailing list.

## BOUNCED MESSAGE

A bounced message is a message that returns to you because it cannot reach its destination. A message usually bounces because of typing mistakes in the e-mail address. Before sending a message, make sure you check the e-mail address for accuracy.

## REPLY TO A MESSAGE

You can reply to a message to answer a question, express an opinion or supply additional information.

### Quoting

When you reply to a message, make sure you include part of the original message. This is called quoting. Quoting helps the reader identify which message you are replying to. To save the reader time, make sure you delete all parts of the original message that do not directly relate to your reply.

## FORWARD A MESSAGE

After reading a message, you can add comments and then send the message to a friend or colleague.

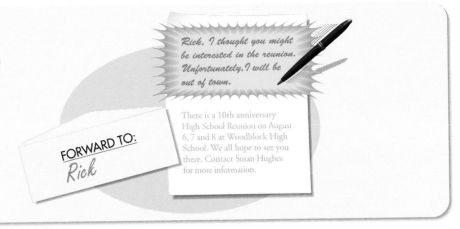

*Rick, I thought you might be interested in the reunion. Unfortunately, I will be out of town.*

There is a 10th anniversary High School Reunion on August 6, 7 and 8 at Woodblock High School. We all hope to see you there. Contact Susan Hughes for more information.

FORWARD TO:
Rick

## ATTACH A FILE TO A MESSAGE

You can attach a document, picture, sound, video or program to a message you are sending. The computer receiving the message must have a program that can view or play the file.

You should try to keep the size of an attached file under 150 KB (Kilobytes), since many computers on the Internet take a long time to transfer messages with large attached files.

### Compress an Attached File

You can use a compression program to shrink the size of a large file you want to attach to an e-mail message. Compressing a file allows the file to transfer more quickly over the Internet. The person receiving a compressed file must also use a compression program to expand the file to its original form.

You can find compression programs at the following Web sites:

**WinZip (Windows)**

www.winzip.com

**StuffIt (Macintosh)**

www.aladdinsys.com/products

To:         jo...
Subject:    Fi...

Congratulations... I'm looking forward to se... at the awards ceremony! I've also included photos from the event in an attached file.

# E-MAIL VIRUSES

E-mail viruses are spread by files attached to e-mail messages. As e-mail attachments become more common, the number of e-mail viruses may also increase.

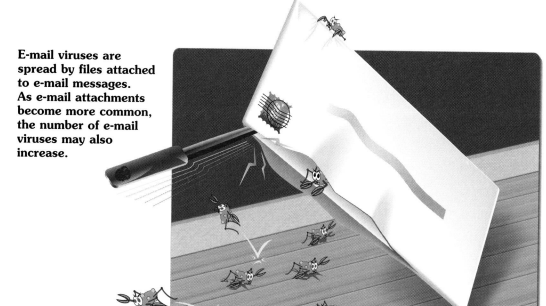

You cannot get an e-mail virus from a message that contains only text.

## VIRUS

A virus is a program that can disrupt the normal operation of a computer. Most viruses are harmless, but some can be destructive. A virus can cause problems such as the appearance of unusual messages on your screen or the destruction of information on your hard drive. Some viruses can affect your computer immediately, while others are set to activate on a certain date.

## HOW E-MAIL VIRUSES SPREAD

When you open an e-mail attachment that contains a virus, the virus spreads to your computer. If you forward the attachment to other people, their computers will also be affected when they open the attachment. Many e-mail viruses can also access your address book and automatically send themselves to the e-mail addresses stored there.

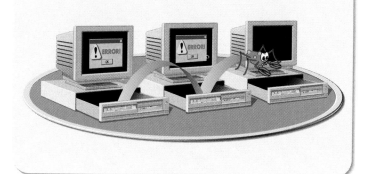

## VIRUS HOAX

A virus hoax is an untrue rumor about a virus. Many e-mail virus warnings on the Internet are virus hoaxes. For example, the Good Times virus is a famous virus hoax that warns people that a virus will infect their computers if they read an e-mail message with the words "good times" in the subject of the message.

## VIRUS SCANNER

A virus scanner is an anti-virus program you can use to check e-mail attachments for viruses. Virus scanner manufacturers regularly release updates that allow their programs to detect the latest known viruses. Always make sure that your virus scanner is up-to-date.

You can find popular virus scanners at the following Web sites:

www.mcafee.com

www.symantec.com/nav

## VIRUS PREVENTION

You should only open e-mail attachments sent by people you trust. If you find an e-mail virus using a virus scanner, you should inform the person who sent you the attachment that their files are infected. This can help stop the spread of the virus.

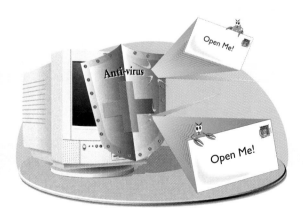

# WEB-BASED E-MAIL

There are several Web sites that allow you to send and receive e-mail on the Web free of charge.

## EASY TO SET UP AND USE

You use your Web browser to send and receive Web-based e-mail. You do not need an e-mail program installed on your computer.

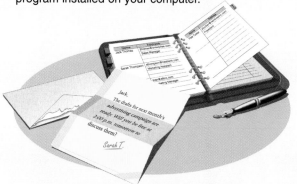

Web-based e-mail is easy to use and works like any e-mail program. You can read and write messages, forward messages to other people and even keep track of your contacts in an address book.

## POPULAR WEB-BASED E-MAIL SERVICES

There are several Web-based e-mail services available. You can find popular Web-based e-mail services at the following Web sites:

www.hotmail.com

www.email.com

mail.yahoo.com

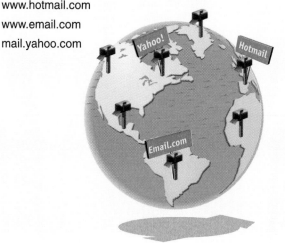

## WORLDWIDE ACCESS

When you use a Web-based e-mail service, you can access your e-mail from any computer in the world that has access to the Web. Web-based e-mail is ideal for people who need access to their e-mail while traveling.

## PERMANENT E-MAIL ADDRESS

Using a Web-based e-mail service allows you to obtain an e-mail address that will not change. This lets you keep the same e-mail address even if you switch to a new Internet access provider.

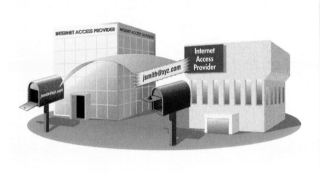

## PRIVATE

To access your e-mail messages from the Web site, you must enter a user name and password for the Web site. Other people cannot access your e-mail account unless you give them your password.

## ACCESS YOUR OTHER ACCOUNTS

Many Web-based e-mail services allow you to access any other e-mail accounts you have set up. For example, you can use your Web-based e-mail service to check for new messages on your e-mail account at work. This allows you to check your business e-mail from any computer with Internet access.

# CHILDREN AND E-MAIL

E-mail is often the easiest way for children to get started using the Internet. You should carefully monitor the e-mail messages your children send and receive.

Children should tell a parent or other adult if they do not feel comfortable about any e-mail messages they receive.

## ADULT SUPERVISION

Constant adult supervision is the best way to ensure that children are not communicating with strangers by e-mail. You should check every e-mail message your children send or receive to make sure they are not communicating with people you are not aware of.

Most e-mail programs allow people to write messages when the computer is not connected to the Internet. This allows you to read your child's messages before connecting to the Internet and sending their messages.

## LIMIT E-MAIL MESSAGES

Many schools allow students to use the computers at school to send and receive e-mail messages. You can restrict your children to exchanging e-mail with their friends and other children they have met at school.

## PERSONAL INFORMATION

Children should never reveal personal information about themselves in e-mail messages, such as which school they attend or where they live. Children should also never mention the location of any clubs or organizations they participate in. Most organizations do not have a security policy and may reveal your address to anyone who contacts the organization.

## FAMILY WEB PAGE

Many families have their own page on the World Wide Web. If your family has a Web page, you should not display your phone number, address or any pictures of your children on the Web page. You also should not place a hyperlink on your family's Web page that allows visitors to send e-mail directly to your children.

## FACE-TO-FACE MEETINGS

Do not allow children to meet friends they have made on the Internet in person without your permission. If a face-to-face meeting is arranged, make sure the meeting is in a public location and a parent or other adult accompanies the child to the meeting.

## CHAPTER 9

# Mailing Lists

*Are you interested in joining a mailing list? This chapter explains how mailing lists work and how to subscribe.*

Mailing List

# INTRODUCTION TO MAILING LISTS

**A mailing list is a discussion group that uses e-mail to communicate.**

There are thousands of mailing lists that cover a wide variety of topics, from aromatherapy to zoology. New mailing lists are created every week.

## HOW MAILING LISTS WORK

When a mailing list receives a message, a copy of the message goes to everyone on the mailing list.

Most mailing lists let you send and receive messages. Some mailing lists only let you receive messages.

## FIND MAILING LISTS

You can find an index of mailing lists at the following Web site:

www.neosoft.com/internet/paml

You can search for mailing lists that discuss a specific topic at the following Web site:

www.liszt.com

## COST

You can join most mailing lists free of charge. Mailing lists that charge people to join are usually used for distributing newsletters and electronic news such as stock market figures.

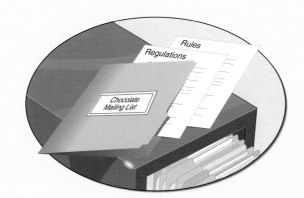

## GET INFORMATION

Before you join a mailing list, try to get as much information as possible about the list. Most mailing lists have their own rules and regulations. Mailing lists often provide an e-mail address where you can send a message to request information about the list.

## START A MAILING LIST

You can start your own mailing list. If only a few people will be using the list, you can run the list with a regular e-mail program on your own computer. Most Internet access providers have programs dedicated to running large mailing lists for their customers. Running your own mailing list can be very time-consuming.

# SUBSCRIBE TO A MAILING LIST

Just as you would subscribe to a newspaper or magazine, you can subscribe to a mailing list that interests you.

Subscribing adds your e-mail address to the mailing list.

## Unsubscribe

If you no longer want to receive messages from a mailing list, you can unsubscribe from the mailing list at any time. Unsubscribing removes your e-mail address from the mailing list.

## MAILING LIST ADDRESSES

Each mailing list has two addresses. Make sure you send your messages to the appropriate address.

### MAILING LIST ADDRESS

The mailing list address receives messages intended for the entire mailing list. This is the address you use to send messages you want all the people on the list to receive. Do not send subscription or unsubscription requests to the mailing list address.

### ADMINISTRATIVE ADDRESS

The administrative address receives messages dealing with administrative issues. This is the address you use to subscribe to or unsubscribe from a mailing list.

### WELCOME MESSAGE

When you subscribe to a mailing list, you usually receive a welcome message to confirm that your e-mail address has been added to the list. This message may also contain information such as rules for sending messages to the list and instructions on how to unsubscribe. You should save the welcome message for future reference.

### CHECK FOR MESSAGES

After you subscribe to a mailing list, make sure you check your mailbox frequently. You can receive dozens of messages in a short period of time.

### DIGESTS

If you receive a lot of messages from a mailing list, find out if the list is available as a digest. A digest groups individual messages together and sends them to you as one message.

### VACATIONS

When you go on vacation, make sure you temporarily unsubscribe from all your mailing lists. This will prevent your mailbox from overflowing with messages.

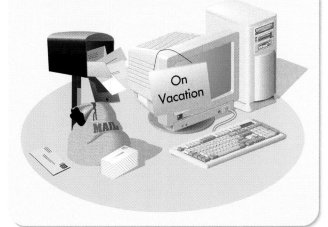

# TYPES OF MAILING LISTS

## MANUALLY MAINTAINED LISTS

A manually maintained mailing list is managed by a person, who is often referred to as the list administrator.

Before you subscribe to a manually maintained list, make sure you find out what information the administrator needs and include the information in your message.

After you subscribe to a manually maintained mailing list, you should start receiving messages from the mailing list within a few days.

## AUTOMATED LISTS

An automated mailing list is managed by a computer program. The three most popular programs for managing automated mailing lists are LISTSERV, Majordomo and ListProc.

The name of the program that manages the mailing list usually appears in the e-mail address you use to subscribe to the list (example:majordomo@hughes.net).

Before you subscribe to an automated list, make sure you find out what information the program needs and include the information in your message. If the program does not understand your message, it may not accept your subscription request.

## RESTRICTED MAILING LISTS

Some mailing lists restrict the number of people allowed to subscribe to the list. If you want to subscribe to one of these lists, you may have to wait for someone else to leave the list.

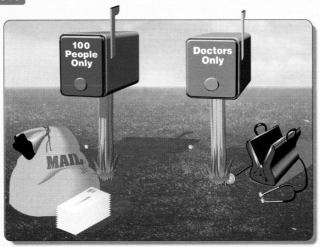

Some mailing lists require that you meet certain qualifications to subscribe to the list. For example, a mailing list about surgery may be restricted to medical doctors.

## MODERATED MAILING LISTS

Some mailing lists are moderated. When a message is sent to a moderated mailing list, a volunteer, referred to as a moderator, reads the message and decides if the message is appropriate and on-topic for the list. If the message is approved, the moderator sends the message to every person on the mailing list.

In an unmoderated mailing list, all messages are automatically sent to everyone on the list. You may have to browse through advertisements and off-topic messages to find messages of interest.

# MAILING LIST ETIQUETTE

Mailing list etiquette refers to the proper way to behave when sending messages to a mailing list.

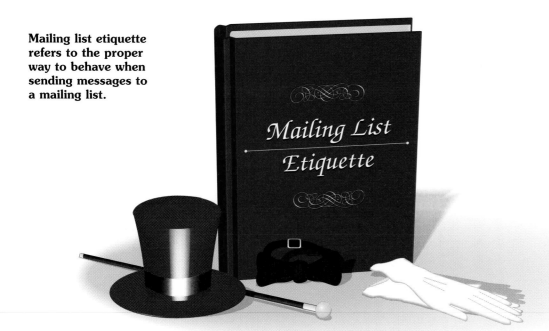

## READ MESSAGES IN THE MAILING LIST

Read the messages in a mailing list for a week before sending a message. This is a good way to learn how people in a mailing list communicate and prevents you from submitting inappropriate information or information already discussed.

## PROOFREAD YOUR MESSAGE

Hundreds of people may read a message you send to a mailing list. Before sending a message, carefully proofread the message for spelling and grammar errors.

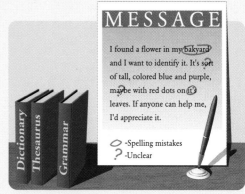

Also make sure your message will not be misinterpreted. For example, not all readers will realize a statement is meant to be sarcastic.

## CHOOSE AN INFORMATIVE SUBJECT

The subject of a message is the first item people read. Make sure the subject clearly identifies the contents of your message. For example, the subject "Read this now" or "For your information" is not very informative.

## REPLY TO MESSAGES

You can reply to a message to answer a question, express an opinion or supply additional information. Reply to a message only when you have something important to say. A reply such as "Me too" or "I agree" is not very useful.

### Quoting

When you reply to a message, make sure you include part of the original message. This is called quoting. Quoting helps readers identify which message you are replying to. To save readers time, make sure you delete all parts of the original message that do not directly relate to your reply.

### Private Replies

If your reply would not be of interest to others in a mailing list or if you want to send a private response, send a reply only to the author of the message.

**Expensive Fishing Equipment**

I really enjoy fishing, but all of my equipment is relatively inexpensive. My fishing buddies keep telling me to upgrade to costly reels and lures. Will this actually make a difference, or is good technique more important than spending lots of money?

B.J. Wilson

**Hot Springs in Arkansas**

My wife and I are planning to take a trip through Arkansas next year. We've heard there are some lovely hot springs in the state, but we don't know where. Could someone please give us some advice?

Thanks, Mark Court

**Footwear**

I am thinking about joining a badminton club at the local gym. Is there special footwear I should buy before I get started? I'm concerned that my old jogging shoes won't quite cut it.

Thanks, J.Martin

Ch

My d
and de
dinner
to go
want a
anyeni

**Mountain Bike Tune-ups**

This is my first year of mountain biking, and so far I've been doing my own tune-ups. But lately my bike hasn't performed well. For example, the chain slips when I switch gears. I'm wondering if I should pay a mechanic to do my tune-ups. Is it worth it?

Thanks, Ronald Hill

**Cactus**

My cactus has gotten too
the pot it is in. Perhaps
could tell me the best w
transplant it.

Thanks, P. C

**Free!**

**Join Now!**

Sunday, August 22, 1999

Bait That Fish Can't Resist

**Free!**

Sunday, August 22, 1999

Royal Wedding

Prince & Princess

Sunday, August 22, 1999

Scientists Find Missing Link

**alt.wedding**

**rec.outdoors.fishing**

**sci.archaeology**

## CHAPTER 10

# Newsgroups

*Do you want to communicate with people on the Internet who share your interests? Find out how to use newsgroups in this chapter.*

# INTRODUCTION TO NEWSGROUPS

A newsgroup is a discussion group that allows people with common interests to communicate with each other.

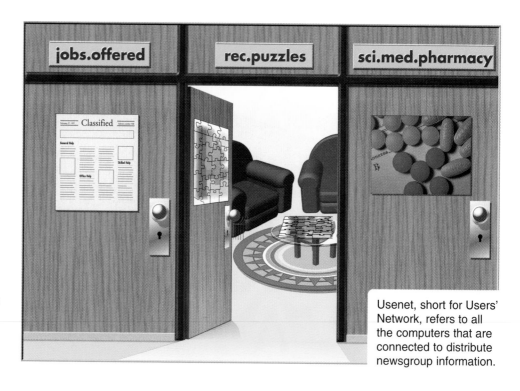

There are thousands of newsgroups on every subject imaginable. Each newsgroup discusses a particular topic such as jobs offered, puzzles or medicine.

Usenet, short for Users' Network, refers to all the computers that are connected to distribute newsgroup information.

## MESSAGES

A newsgroup can contain hundreds or thousands of messages.

**Message**

A message is information that an individual posts, or sends, to a newsgroup. A message can be a few lines of text or the length of a book. Messages are also called articles.

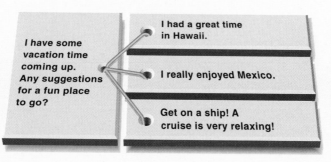

**Thread**

A thread is a message and all replies to the message. A thread may include an initial question and the responses from other readers. A thread can help you keep track of all the replies to a message.

## NEWSGROUP NAMES

The name of a newsgroup describes the type of information discussed in the newsgroup. A newsgroup name consists of two or more words, separated by periods (.).

**rec.sport.basketball.pro**

The first word describes the main topic (example: rec for recreation). Each of the following words narrows the topic.

## NEWSGROUP CATEGORIES

Newsgroups are divided into sections, or categories. The newsgroups in each category discuss the same general topic.

### Main Newsgroup Categories

| Category | Topic |
|----------|-------|
| alt | General interest |
| biz | Business |
| comp | Computers |
| rec | Recreation and hobbies |
| sci | Science |
| soc | Social (culture and politics) |
| misc | Miscellaneous |
| talk | Debate |

**nyc.politics**

You can also find newsgroup categories that focus on specific subjects, such as companies or geographic locations. For example, you can find newsgroups that discuss only Microsoft products (example: microsoft.public.win98.internet) or newsgroups that discuss issues about your city or state (example: nyc.politics).

# NEWSREADERS

A newsreader is a program that lets you read and post messages to newsgroups.

Some Web browsers come with a built-in newsreader. Newsreaders built into Web browsers often do not have as many features as separate newsreader programs.

## POPULAR NEWSREADERS

Some popular newsreaders include the following:

**Free Agent (Windows)**

www.forteinc.com/agent

**Gravity (Windows)**

www.microplanet.com

**NewsWatcher (Macintosh)**

www.macorchard.com/usenet.html

**Gravity**

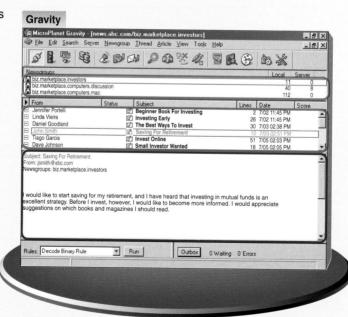

■ This area displays a list of newsgroups.

■ This area displays a list of all the messages in the selected newsgroup.

■ This area displays the contents of a single message.

**NEWSREADER FEATURES**

## KILL FILES

Most newsreaders allow you to create a kill file that stores the names of people whose messages you do not want to read. The newsreader will automatically delete any messages posted by a person listed in the kill file. This is useful when someone is frequently posting inappropriate messages to a newsgroup.

## SORT MESSAGES

When displaying messages in a newsgroup, you can usually view information about each message, such as the author's name, the subject of the message and the date the message was sent to the newsgroup. Most newsreaders automatically sort messages by date, but you can sort by other information to help you find messages of interest.

## FILTERS

Many newsreaders provide filters that allow you to display only the type of messages you want to read. This lets you find the information you need without having to read every message in the newsgroup.

## PRIVACY

There are many companies that index all messages posted to Usenet newsgroups. This allows people on the Internet to search the indexed messages and monitor which newsgroups you post to and how often you post messages. To keep your messages private, some newsreaders now let you automatically mark a message so search companies cannot index the message.

# SUBSCRIBE TO NEWSGROUPS

You subscribe to a newsgroup you want to read on a regular basis. If you no longer want to read the messages in a newsgroup, you can unsubscribe from the newsgroup at any time.

## NEW NEWSGROUPS

New newsgroups are created every day. A newsreader lets you display a list of all the newsgroups that have been created since the last time you checked. Once you have the list of new newsgroups, you can subscribe to a new newsgroup of interest.

1. alt.comics.dilbert
2. comp.music.misc
3. rec.scuba.locations
4. rec.travel.africa
5. soc.culture.kenya

## SIMILAR NEWSGROUPS

There is often more than one newsgroup for a topic. For example, the topics discussed in the **alt.books.reviews** newsgroup are similar to the topics discussed in **rec.arts.books**. If you are interested in a specific topic, you may want to subscribe to all the newsgroups that discuss the topic.

Similar Newsgroups

alt.autos
rec.autos
alt.cars

## MODERATED NEWSGROUPS

Some newsgroups are moderated. In these newsgroups, a volunteer reads each message and decides if the message is appropriate for the newsgroup. The volunteer then posts the approved messages for everyone to read.

Moderated newsgroups may have the word "moderated" at the end of the newsgroup name (example: misc.taxes.moderated).

**A news server is a computer that stores newsgroup messages.**

Most news servers are maintained by Internet access providers, which are companies that give you access to the Internet. The newsgroups available to you depend on your access provider. Your access provider may limit the available newsgroups to save valuable storage space.

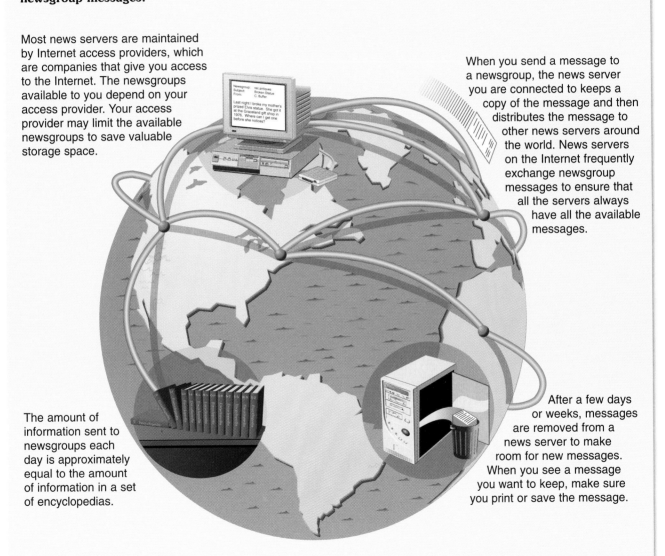

When you send a message to a newsgroup, the news server you are connected to keeps a copy of the message and then distributes the message to other news servers around the world. News servers on the Internet frequently exchange newsgroup messages to ensure that all the servers always have all the available messages.

The amount of information sent to newsgroups each day is approximately equal to the amount of information in a set of encyclopedias.

After a few days or weeks, messages are removed from a news server to make room for new messages. When you see a message you want to keep, make sure you print or save the message.

# WORK WITH NEWSGROUP MESSAGES

## REPLY TO A MESSAGE

You can reply to a message to answer a question, express an opinion or supply additional information. A reply you post to a newsgroup is called a follow-up.

### Quote Original Message

When you reply to a message, make sure you include part of the original message. This is called quoting. Quoting helps readers identify which message you are replying to. To save readers time, make sure you delete all parts of the original message that do not directly relate to your reply.

### Send a Private Reply

You can send a reply to the author of a message, the entire newsgroup or both. If your reply would not be of interest to others in a newsgroup or if you want to send a private reply, send a message only to the author of the message.

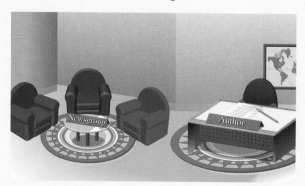

### Verify E-mail Address

To avoid receiving junk e-mail, some people make small changes to their e-mail address in their newsgroup messages, such as typing "at" instead of the @ symbol. Before sending a private reply to the author of a message, make sure you correct any intentional changes in the author's e-mail address.

## POST A MESSAGE

You can post, or send, a new message to a newsgroup to ask a question or express an opinion. Thousands of people around the world may read a message you post.

If you want to practice posting a message, send a message to the **alt.test** newsgroup. You will receive an automated reply to let you know you posted correctly. Do not send practice messages to other newsgroups.

## ATTACH PICTURES AND PROGRAMS

You can share pictures and programs with other people in a newsgroup. When you attach a picture or program to a message you post, your newsreader will automatically change the picture or program into a binary file. Binary files transfer easily over the Internet.

There are many newsgroups available for people who want to exchange binary files. Most newsgroups that accept binary files have the word "binaries" in the name (example: alt.binaries.clip-art). Before you attach a picture or program to a newsgroup message, check the FAQ for the newsgroup to see if there are any restrictions on binary files.

# NEWSGROUP ETIQUETTE

## READ MESSAGES

Read the messages in a newsgroup for a week before posting a message. This is called lurking. Lurking is a good way to learn how people in a newsgroup communicate and prevents you from posting information others have already read.

## READ THE FAQ

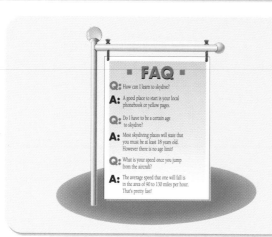

The FAQ (Frequently Asked Questions) is a document containing a list of questions and answers that often appear in a newsgroup. The FAQ is designed to prevent new readers from asking questions that have already been answered. Make sure you read the FAQ before posting any messages to a newsgroup.

## CHOOSE AN INFORMATIVE SUBJECT

The subject of a message is the first item people read. Make sure your subject clearly identifies the contents of your message. For example, the subject "Read this now" or "For your information" is not very informative.

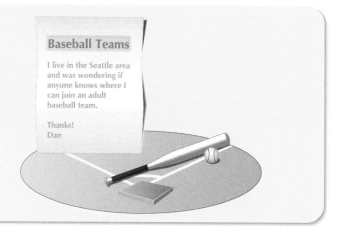

## PROOFREAD YOUR MESSAGES

Thousands of people around the world may read a message you post to a newsgroup. Before posting a message, make sure the message is clear, concise and contains no spelling or grammar errors. Also make sure your message will not be misinterpreted. For example, not all readers will realize a statement is meant to be sarcastic.

### MESSAGE

I just won the lottery. I bought a new Pentium computer. I want to buy a new printer to go with it. Does anyone has any suggestions? Price is probably not an issue but it might be. I would prefer something that are fast, reliable and can print in full color. Thanks in advance.

⬯ -Grammar errors

? -Misleading

## AVOID FLAMES

A flame is an angry or insulting message directed at one person. A flame war is an argument that continues for a while. Avoid starting or participating in flame wars.

## POST TO THE APPROPRIATE NEWSGROUP

Make sure you post a message to the appropriate newsgroup. This ensures that people interested in your questions and comments will see your message.

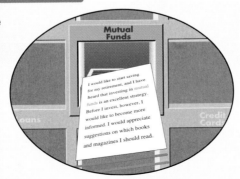

Do not post a message to several inappropriate newsgroups. This is called spamming. Spamming is particularly annoying when the message serves a commercial purpose, such as selling a product or service.

# FIND NEWSGROUP MESSAGES

**Deja.com is a Web site that makes it easy to find messages people have posted to newsgroups.**

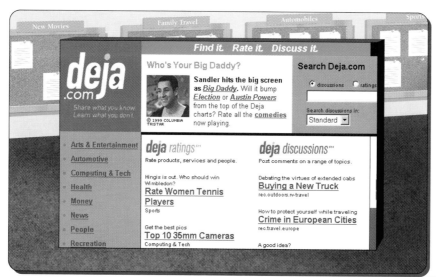

You can find Deja.com at the following Web site:

www.deja.com

## AVAILABLE MESSAGES

Deja.com uses a database to store messages that are posted to more than 45,000 newsgroups. The database currently contains more than 300 million messages dating back to March 1995.

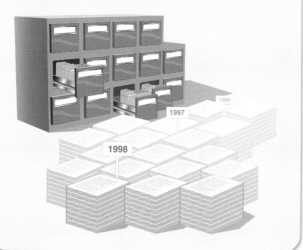

## KEEP MESSAGES PRIVATE

When a message is stored in Deja.com's database, anyone using Deja.com can find and read the message. If you do not want people using Deja.com to find messages you post to a newsgroup, you can prevent Deja.com from storing your messages. Before you send a message to a newsgroup, type **x-no-archive: yes** in the first line of the message.

## SIMPLE SEARCH

Performing a simple search is the fastest and easiest way to search for messages at Deja.com. When you enter words in the search area, Deja.com searches its database and displays a list of messages containing all the words you specified.

You can read messages displayed in the list and even send an e-mail message to the author of a message. Simple searches only search messages posted to newsgroups in the last several weeks.

## POWER SEARCH

The Power Search provides many options you can use to narrow your search. Using the Power Search, you can search through all the messages stored in the Deja.com database. You can also search for messages written by a specific person or indicate how you want to sort the search results.

## AUTHOR POSTING HISTORY

You can use Deja.com to find information about people who have posted messages to newsgroups. After you read a message you have found, you can display the posting history of the author. This allows you to see which newsgroups the author has posted messages to in the past and review the other messages.

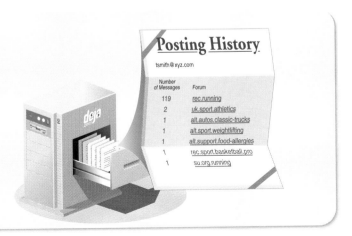

# WEB-BASED DISCUSSION GROUPS

Many Web sites offer discussion groups that you can participate in. These Web-based discussion groups, also called forums, are not part of the Usenet newsgroups.

You use your Web browser to participate in Web-based discussion groups. You do not need a newsreader program.

## USER NAME AND PASSWORD

You may need to enter a user name and password to access some Web-based discussion groups. This allows the people who created the discussion group to monitor the discussions. A person who frequently posts off-topic or offensive messages may be banned from the discussion group.

## IMAGES AND ANIMATION

Unlike newsreader programs, Web browsers can display multimedia, so many Web-based discussion groups allow you to include images and animation in your messages.

## WHERE TO FIND WEB-BASED DISCUSSION GROUPS

### DISCUSSION GROUP WEB SITES

There are several Web sites that offer access to many discussion groups. The discussion groups are often grouped into categories, such as health, entertainment or travel. You can also search for discussion groups on a topic of interest.

The following Web sites offer access to many discussion groups:

www.deja.com

www.delphi.com

www.forumone.com

### COMPANY WEB SITES

Companies often set up discussion groups on their Web sites to promote their products, provide technical support and receive and respond to customer feedback. Companies may also set up private Web-based discussion groups to hold meetings with participants who are in different locations.

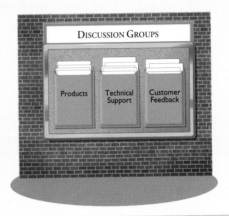

### GENERAL WEB SITES

Many general interest Web sites have their own discussion groups that allow visitors to discuss the topic of the Web site. For example, a fitness Web site may provide a discussion group that lets visitors ask questions and discuss the latest fitness trends.

Some newspaper and magazine Web sites also provide discussion groups for visitors to discuss current issues, such as politics or sports.

# CHILDREN AND NEWSGROUPS

There are many newsgroups that children can participate in to discuss topics such as pets, sports and hobbies. You should closely monitor any newsgroups your children subscribe to.

alt.kids-talk
alt.tv.simpsons
rec.toys.misc
alt.tv.muppets

## ADULT SUPERVISION

Constant adult supervision is the best way to ensure that children do not access inappropriate information in newsgroups. You should read all the messages in a newsgroup for a week before you let your children access the newsgroup.

## SELECT NEWSGROUPS

If your newsreader allows you to read and compose messages offline, you can control which newsgroups your children access and which messages they respond to. You can get messages from only the newsgroups you feel are appropriate for children. After the children have read the messages and written replies, you can read the replies before connecting to the Internet and sending their messages.

## PERSONAL INFORMATION

Children should never include personal information about themselves in a message they post to a newsgroup, such as their name, address or which school they attend. Children should also never mention the location of any clubs or organizations they participate in. Most organizations do not have a security policy and may reveal the child's address to anyone who contacts the organization.

## POST ANONYMOUSLY

Many newsreaders let you use a nickname and fake e-mail address when posting messages to a newsgroup. If children want to participate in a newsgroup that is not specifically for children, they should use a phony name and e-mail address so they do not reveal their true identity.

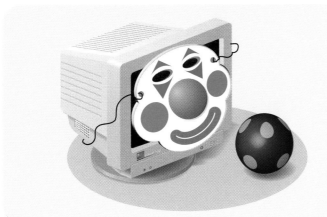

## E-MAIL RESPONSES

When you post a message to a newsgroup, you often receive e-mail messages from people commenting on the message. Children should ignore any information in an e-mail reply that does not directly relate to the information in the message you posted. If a child receives an inappropriate e-mail message, they should not respond to the message.

## CHAPTER 11

# Chat

*Would you like to chat with other people on the Internet? This chapter introduces you to Internet Relay Chat, Web-based chat and much more.*

# INTRODUCTION TO CHAT

You can instantly communicate with people around the world by typing back and forth. This is called chatting.

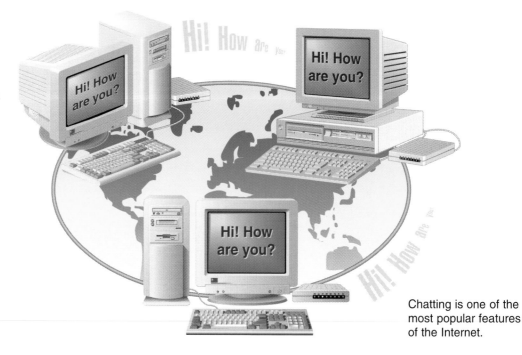

Chatting is one of the most popular features of the Internet.

## TYPES OF CHAT

### TEXT-BASED

Text-based chat is the oldest and most popular type of chat on the Internet. You can have conversations with one or more people. When chatting, the text you type immediately appears on the screen of each person participating in the conversation. Since text transfers quickly over the Internet, you do not need a high-speed connection to the Internet to participate in text-based chat.

> Tanya - I need some help! I have to write an essay about an unusual animal. Any ideas?
>
> Chris - How about the dodo bird?
>
> Robin - My teacher assigned me the same project and I couldn't find any info on the dodo bird.
>
> Chris - What animal did you write about?
>
> Robin - I wrote about the sea cucumber. It's unusual and there is lots of info out there.

### MULTIMEDIA

Multimedia chat allows you to have voice conversations and communicate through live video over the Internet. Since sound and video transfer slowly over the Internet, you should have a high-speed connection to the Internet to use multimedia chat.

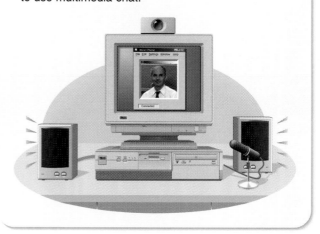

**REASONS FOR CHAT**

### EDUCATION

Many students use chat to discuss assignments and get help from instructors and fellow students. This is particularly useful for people who are too far away from schools or colleges to attend classes on a regular basis.

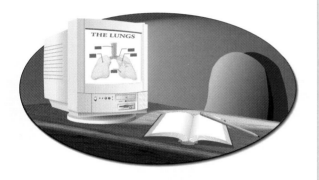

### ENTERTAINMENT

Most people use chat as a form of entertainment. You can use chat to meet new friends from all over the world.

### KEEP IN TOUCH

Chatting is a low-cost way to stay in touch with friends or relatives who have access to the Internet. Many people use chat to communicate with family, friends and colleagues in other cities, states or countries without paying long distance telephone charges.

### PRODUCT SUPPORT

Some product manufacturers use chat to provide technical support for their customers. Technical support people make themselves available for chatting so customers can ask questions and get answers instantly.

# INTERNET RELAY CHAT

Internet Relay Chat (IRC) is a system that allows you to chat with other people on the Internet.

**IRC Chat**

| | |
|---|---|
| \<Greg\> | I would like to fill my apartment with plants but I have such a hard time growing them. I certainly wasn't born with a green thumb. |
| \<Brenda\> | Well, why don't you buy a cactus? They are easy to grow. |
| \<John\> | I agree. A cactus is simple to care for. It only needs water once a month. |
| \<Michael\> | And a cactus will grow well with little light. |
| \<Greg\> | If I decide to buy a cactus, what kind should I choose? |
| \<Michael\> | Well, I like the Desert Gold variety. |
| \<John\> | Yes, they're attractive. But handle with care; their spines are quite sharp. |
| \<Greg\> | Great, the only plant I can grow is the kind that bites! |

To use IRC, you must connect to a computer called an IRC server. Each IRC server is connected to a network of other IRC servers around the world.

## NAME AND E-MAIL ADDRESS

Before connecting to IRC, you must enter your name and e-mail address. Most IRC servers will not let you connect unless you enter a valid e-mail address. You can enter a fake name if you wish to remain anonymous, but other people may still be able to find out your real name.

## NICKNAME

You must choose a nickname for yourself before using IRC. If another person is already using your nickname, you must choose a different nickname. Some IRC servers limit the number of characters you can have in your nickname. You may be able to register your nickname so no one else can use the nickname.

## IRC CHANNELS

There are many channels, or chat groups, you can join on IRC. Each channel usually focuses on a specific topic. A channel name often tells you the theme of the discussion.

A # symbol in front of a channel name means the channel is available to people all over the world.

In addition to the many channels available on IRC, you can create your own channel and invite other people to chat with you there.

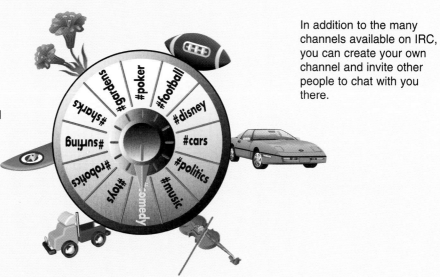

## IRC PROGRAMS

You need an IRC program to be able to connect to an IRC server. Most IRC programs are very easy to use and provide many features that you can customize to suit your needs. For example, some IRC programs allow you to change the font and color of the text that appears on your screen to make the text easier to read.

You can find free trial versions of IRC programs at the following Web sites:

**mIRC (Windows)**

www.mirc.com

**Ircle (Macintosh)**

www.ircle.com

# WEB-BASED CHAT

Web-based chat is a popular feature of the Internet. Web-based chat is fun and easy to use.

## WEB BROWSER

Most of the chat networks on the World Wide Web require only that you have a Web browser to participate. Some Web-based chat networks use Java to display the discussion in the chat room on your screen. If you have trouble participating in a Web-based chat network, make sure you have the latest version of your Web browser.

## REGISTRATION

You can use most of the chat services on the Web for free. Many Web-based chat networks require that you register with the Web site before you can enter the chat rooms. To register, you must enter information such as your name and e-mail address. You may also be asked to enter a user name and password each time you use the chat network.

## CHAT WEB SITES

### WBS

WBS (WebChat Broadcasting System) claims to be one of the largest Web-based chat networks on the Internet. WBS offers chat rooms on many topics, including romance, music, sports and education. You can access the WBS chat network at the following Web site:

www.wbs.net

### TALK CITY

Talk City is a popular Web-based chat network. Talk City chat rooms are well organized so you can easily find chat rooms for topics that interest you. Talk City also offers scheduled chats hosted by celebrities, such as authors and athletes. You can access the Talk City chat network at the following Web site:

www.talkcity.com

## 3D CHAT

### WORLDS ULTIMATE 3D CHAT PLUS

Worlds Ultimate 3D Chat Plus allows you to walk around and talk to other people in a three-dimensional world. Objects such as penguins and chess pieces represent the people in a 3D chat room. These objects are called avatars.

You must have the Worlds Ultimate 3D Chat Plus software before you can participate in the 3D chat. You can find a free version of the Worlds Ultimate 3D Chat Plus software at the following Web site:

www.worlds.net

# VOICE AND VIDEO CHAT

With voice and video chat, you can hear and see friends, family members and colleagues, even if they are on the other side of the world.

Voice and video chat over the Internet let you communicate with other people without paying any long distance telephone charges.

## EQUIPMENT

To talk to other people on the Internet, you must have a sound card installed on your computer with speakers and a microphone attached.

If you want other people to see you while you are chatting, you must connect a video camera to your computer. You can buy an inexpensive video camera that attaches to the top of your monitor. You can also use a regular video camera if you have a video capture card installed on your computer.

## VOICE AND VIDEO CHAT PROGRAMS

You need a special program to hear and see people while chatting on the Internet. You can get voice and video chat programs at the following Web sites:

**Create & Share**
www.intel.com/createshare

**Internet Phone**
www.vocaltec.com/products

**CU-SeeMe**
www.wpine.com

## CONTACT OTHER PEOPLE

If you want to communicate with another person using voice or video chat, you both may need to use the same type of voice or video chat program. You can usually find a directory of people who use your program at the Web site where you got the program. You can search the directory to find people you want to chat with.

## IMAGE QUALITY

If you are using a modem to transfer video images, the quality of the images may be poor. Some video chat programs can help increase the quality of video images. If possible, you should try out a video chat program to see the quality of the images before purchasing the program.

# CHAT ETIQUETTE

Just like at a cocktail party, there is a proper way to behave when chatting with people on the Internet.

If you do not respect the rules in a chat room, you could be banned from chatting in the room in the future.

## RESPECT LANGUAGE

People from many different countries use chat to communicate. This means many chat rooms might be used by people who do not speak the same language as you. When you join a chat room, respect the language being used in the room. If you want to discuss the topic in your own language, you may be able to start a new room for people who speak the same language as you.

## AVOID OFFENSIVE LANGUAGE

Keep in mind that people of all ages and backgrounds use chat rooms. When chatting, do not use offensive language or annoy other people in the chat room. If another person is annoying you or using offensive language, you should ignore them.

## WRITING STYLE

You do not have to use proper punctuation or capitalization when chatting, but make sure you do not type in all UPPERCASE LETTERS. This is called shouting and is considered rude. You should also try to keep your messages short, as you would in a real conversation. Shorter messages help keep the conversation flowing.

## READ CONVERSATION BEFORE PARTICIPATING

When you first enter a chat room, read the conversation in progress for a moment. This allows you to understand what is going on in the chat room before you begin participating.

## USE COMMON SENSE

When chatting, do not reveal too much information about yourself, such as your e-mail address, phone number, password or credit card number. Remember that people in a chat room are not always who they say they are.

## DO NOT ADVERTISE

You should never enter a chat room with the intention of promoting your business, product or services. In most cases, people in a chat room are interested in talking with other people, not reading advertisements.

# CHILDREN AND CHAT

There are many chat rooms available where children can discuss topics such as television shows, music and school. You should closely monitor any chat rooms your children participate in.

## ADULT SUPERVISION

Constant adult supervision is the best way to ensure that children do not participate in inappropriate conversations in a chat room. You may want to keep the computer in the family room or kitchen so you can monitor the conversations in the chat room.

## SET GUIDELINES

Before a child spends time in a chat room, discuss which types of information are acceptable and which types of information to be wary of. Children should tell a parent or other adult if they do not feel comfortable about any conversations in a chat room they participate in.

Guidelines

- No foul language
- No X-rated Web sites
- Do not give personal information to strangers

## CHAT ANONYMOUSLY

When chatting on the Internet, children should use a fake nickname so they do not reveal their true identity. Children should not provide information such as their real name, e-mail address or telephone number to anyone in a chat room. Children should also never reveal personal information, such as which school they attend or where they live.

> <Mary> Hi, my name is Mary. I am 12 years old. How old are you?

## BE CAREFUL

Children should keep in mind that people may not be who they say they are in a chat room. For example, someone who says she is a 12-year old girl may be a 40-year old man. Children should always be careful of who they chat with and the information they give out.

## POPULAR WEB-BASED CHAT ROOMS

There are many chat rooms on the Internet that children can participate in. You can find some chat rooms designed especially for children and teenagers at the following Web sites:

chat.freezone.com

www.headbone.com/chat

# INSTANT MESSAGES

You can exchange instant messages to have a private conversation with friends, colleagues and family members on the Internet.

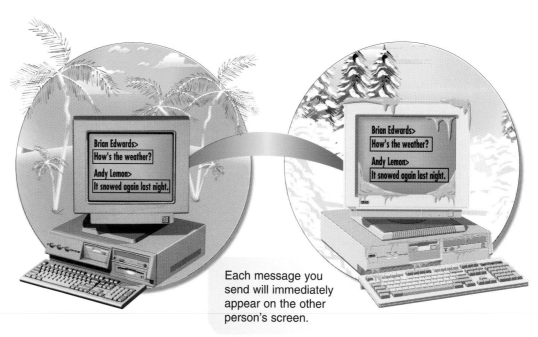

Each message you send will immediately appear on the other person's screen.

## INSTANT MESSAGING PROGRAMS

You need to install an instant messaging program on your computer to exchange instant messages with other people.
You and the people you want to exchange messages with must use compatible instant messaging programs. You can find popular instant messaging programs at the following Web sites:

**ICQ**

www.icq.com

**AOL Instant Messenger**

www.aol.com/aim

**MSN Messenger**

messenger.msn.com

### Contact List

Instant messaging programs provide a contact list where you can save the identities of people you frequently exchange messages with. After you add a person to your contact list, your instant messaging program will notify you when the person goes online.

## REASONS FOR INSTANT MESSAGES

### SAVE MONEY

Sending instant messages is a great way to communicate with family and friends around the world without paying long distance telephone charges.

### COMMUNICATE WITH COLLEAGUES

Sending instant messages is ideal for companies that have employees located in different offices or employees who work from home. Employees can use instant messages to find out when others are online and easily communicate with them. Using instant messages is more convenient than leaving phone messages.

### FIND NEW FRIENDS

You can find new friends on the Internet who use an instant messaging program. When people register with an instant messaging program, they can enter information about themselves, such as their occupation, hobbies and interests. You can use this information to find and then communicate with people who share your interests.

## CHAPTER 12

# Multi-Player Games

*Are you interested in playing games on the Internet? This chapter will help you get started.*

# INTRODUCTION TO MULTI-PLAYER GAMES

A multi-player game is a game that lets you use a computer to play against one or more opponents. Multi-player games are becoming one of the most popular uses of the Internet.

You can play board games, card games, trivia games, arcade-style games and fast-paced action or adventure games.

## SOFTWARE REQUIREMENTS

Most multi-player games on the Internet require that you have software for the game installed on your computer. You can download software for many games from the Internet for free. To play some games on the Internet, you must first buy the CD-ROM version of the game.

## WEB SITES

There are many multi-player game Web sites available where you can play games with other people on the Internet, chat about your favorite games and learn about the latest tips and tricks.

Some popular game Web sites include:

www.zone.com

www.won.net

## MULTI-PLAYER GAME ADVANTAGES

### FLEXIBLE

There are hundreds of multi-player games you can play over the Internet. Everyone can find a game that suits their interests. You can choose from simple card games to complex games requiring science and math skills.

### INTERACTIVE

Playing multi-player games on the Internet allows you to interact and communicate with people from all over the world. Some games even have their own associations where players can meet each other face to face.

### CHALLENGING

Even though you can play most games against a computer, many games are better when you play them against other people. Most computers react the same way each time you play a game. When you play a game against a person, the game will be different every time.

### COMPETITIVE

Playing games on the Internet can be very competitive. Almost every game played on the Internet has a site on the World Wide Web that displays a list of winners. Some games even have tournaments for the top players.

# PLAY BY E-MAIL GAMES

Play By E-Mail (PBEM) games are a convenient, simple way to participate in multi-player games. To play an e-mail game, you need an e-mail account set up on your computer.

Move 10:
White bishop C2 to B3

## TYPES OF GAMES

There are several types of e-mail games. To play the simplest type, such as chess or checkers, you exchange moves with your opponent by e-mail. In more complex types of games, all the players e-mail their moves to one computer. The computer processes all the moves and controls the flow of the game.

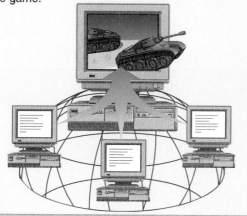

## BENEFITS

E-mail games allow each player to play at a convenient time, so you do not have to constantly be at your computer to play. You can also easily find an opponent whose skill level matches your skill level. Playing against people with similar skill levels usually makes games more fun.

Sink & Destroy

Find a player at your skill level!

Beginner | Intermediate
Steven | Treena
Sean | Russ
Peter | Jamie

Advanced
Jimmy
Roxanne

## GLOBAL DIPLOMACY

Global Diplomacy is a strategy game where you attempt to conquer the world by negotiating with other players. You can find Global Diplomacy at the following Web site:

www.islandnet.com/~dgreenin/emg-game.htm#GD

## FOOD CHAIN

This mathematics-based game allows you to design a species of animal and then release it into the jungle, where the species will either survive or become extinct. You can find Food Chain at the following Web site:

www.pbm.com/~lindahl/fchain.html

## ELECTRONIC KNOCK OUT

In this game, you are the manager of a boxer. You submit your boxer for fights against other boxers and control the characteristics of your boxer. You can find Electronic Knock Out at the following Web site:

www.boxinggame.com

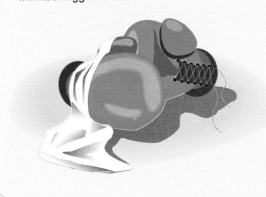

## E-MAIL AMERICAN CIVIL WAR

In this strategy game, you communicate with other players to plan your attacks and attempt to defeat your opponent in the American Civil War. You can find E-mail American Civil War at the following Web site:

www.teleport.com/~stank

# TRADITIONAL MULTI-PLAYER GAMES

Some of the first games played on the Internet were traditional board and card games, such as backgammon and bridge.

## PLAYERS

When you play traditional multi-player board games or card games on the Internet, you can quickly find opponents and start a game. You can usually find an opponent whose skill level matches your skill level. You can also organize games with friends or family members, even if they are located on the other side of the world.

## BOARD GAMES

Many people find it difficult to play a board game when the board is displayed on a computer screen. To avoid this problem, you can set up the game board in front of your computer. You can then move the game pieces on the board according to what appears on your computer screen.

## TRADITIONAL GAMES

### BACKGAMMON

There are many places on the Internet where you can play backgammon. Many Web sites offer information about playing backgammon on the Internet, such as the rules, where to play against other people and much more. You can find information about backgammon at the following Web site:

www.bkgm.com

### BRIDGE

Bridge is one of the most popular card games in the world. You can use the Internet to learn and practice the game. When you are ready to play against real people, you can easily find opponents on the Internet. You can find information about bridge at the following Web site:

www.bridgeplayer.com

### CHESS

Chess is one of the oldest games in the world. The Internet Chess Club provides information on the game and hosts over 60,000 chess matches each day. The Internet Chess Club is located at the following Web site:

www.chessclub.com

### HEARTS

Hearts is one of the most popular card games on the Internet. There are many Web sites that let you play Hearts with other people on the Internet. You can find information about Hearts at the following Web site:

www.pagat.com/reverse/hearts.html

# COMMERCIAL SOFTWARE GAMES

You can buy commercial software games at most computer stores and on the Internet. Many commercial software games allow you to play against other people on the Internet.

## SOFTWARE REQUIREMENTS

When playing a commercial software game with other people on the Internet, each person must have their own copy of the game. Commercial software games can be expensive, but manufacturers often offer a free trial version of the software on the Web.

## HARDWARE REQUIREMENTS

Some games require hardware that allows you to interact with the game, such as a joystick or gamepad. You may also need hardware that helps the game run better. For example, many commercial software games run best on computers with 3-D graphics cards installed. Before buying a game, check the system requirements of the game.

## CONNECTING

Connecting to other people on the Internet to play a commercial software game is often very simple. You can usually connect to a computer on the Internet that allows you to contact and play with other people.

## POPULAR COMMERCIAL GAMES

### AGE OF EMPIRES

Age of Empires is a strategy game that spans ten thousand years and allows you to rewrite the history of civilization. You can find more information about Age of Empires at the following Web site:

www.microsoft.com/games/empires

### COMMAND & CONQUER

Command & Conquer is a military strategy game you can play with another person on the Internet. You can find more information about Command & Conquer at the following Web site:

www.westwood.com

### JEDI KNIGHT: DARK FORCES II

In this Star Wars® game, you can use your lightsaber to battle the evil Empire. You can play with up to three other people on the Internet at once. You can find more information about Jedi Knight at the following Web site:

www.lucasarts.com/static/jk

### NEED FOR SPEED: HIGH STAKES

Need for Speed: High Stakes allows you to choose your dream car and race against another player. You can find more information about Need for Speed at the following Web site:

www.needforspeed.com

## CHAPTER 13

# Intranets

*Would you like to learn about intranets? Read this chapter to find out about intranet features, security and more.*

# INTRODUCTION TO NETWORKS

A network is a group of connected computers that allows people to share information and equipment.

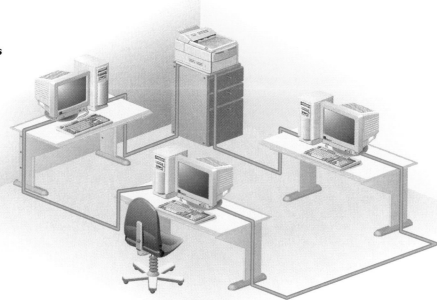

## TYPES OF NETWORKS

### LOCAL AREA NETWORK

A Local Area Network (LAN) is a network that connects computers within a small geographic area, such as a building.

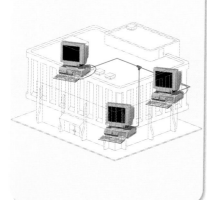

### WIDE AREA NETWORK

A Wide Area Network (WAN) is a network that connects computers across a large geographic area, such as a city or country. The Internet is a WAN.

## NETWORK OPERATING SYSTEM

A Network Operating System (NOS) is designed for powerful computers, called network servers, to ensure that all parts of a network work together smoothly and efficiently. A network operating system allows a network server to store programs and information so other computers on the network can access the programs and information.

## NETWORK ADVANTAGES

### WORK AWAY FROM OFFICE

When traveling or at home, you can connect to the network at work to exchange messages and files.

### ELIMINATE SNEAKERNET

Sneakernet refers to physically carrying information from one computer to another to exchange information. A computer network eliminates the need for sneakernet.

### SHARE INFORMATION

Networks let you easily share information and programs. You can exchange documents, electronic mail, video, sound and images.

### SHARE EQUIPMENT

Computers connected to a network can share equipment, such as a printer or modem.

## NETWORK ADMINISTRATOR

A network administrator manages the network and makes sure the network runs smoothly. A network administrator may also be called a network manager, information systems manager or system administrator.

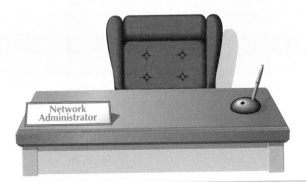

# INTRODUCTION TO INTRANETS

An intranet is a network, similar to the Internet, within a company or organization.

## INTERNET TECHNOLOGY

Intranets transfer information on a network using the same technology that is used to transfer information on the Internet. This allows intranets to exchange information quickly and easily on different types of networks without having to consider the operating systems used on each network.

## SERVERS

Intranets use special computers, called servers, to control the distribution of information on an intranet. On most intranets, one server is connected to the network for each intranet feature required, such as an e-mail or Web system. Many intranet servers are similar to the servers used on the Internet.

## SOFTWARE

The software used to exchange information on an intranet, such as a Web browser or e-mail reader, is the same as the software used to exchange information on the Internet. Most required software is available at computer stores or on the Internet.

## INFORMATION

Many software programs allow people on an intranet to provide information from their own computers to other people on the intranet. For example, before going on vacation, an employee could create a personal Web page for others to read. Information on the page could include emergency contacts and the days the employee will be absent.

## EFFICIENCY

Intranets allow employees of a company or organization to access information quickly and efficiently. When information is easy to access, it often increases the productivity of the employees. For example, employees can access a phone directory on the intranet instead of contacting the receptionist for numbers.

# INTRANET FEATURES

Intranets offer many of the features and services that are available on the Internet.

## MULTIMEDIA

Information transfers much faster over an intranet than over the Internet. This makes it easy to transfer sound and video files that would take too long to transfer over the Internet. You can use an intranet to easily distribute product demonstrations and training videos to anyone connected to the intranet.

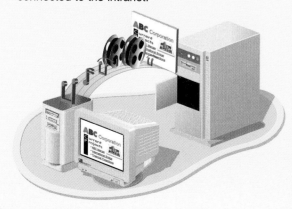

## FILE SHARING

File sharing is one of the main reasons a company or organization would set up an intranet. You can place documents on an intranet that you would not display on the Internet, such as workplace procedures or a company newsletter.

Employees can also use an intranet to update or install new software programs. Transferring software from an intranet to your computer is much easier than using floppy disks or CD-ROM discs.

## E-MAIL

Some companies use e-mail systems that only allow employees to exchange simple text. Intranets allow companies to use the same type of e-mail system that is found on the Internet. This lets employees send much more information in an e-mail message, such as a spreadsheet or a word processing document.

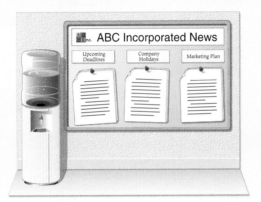

## NEWSGROUPS

Many organizations use newsgroups that are similar to the Usenet newsgroups found on the Internet. Employees can use newsgroups to share information about the company or about a specific project. People can post questions or updates to the newsgroups so their colleagues can view the information.

## CHAT

Companies can set up chat channels, or groups, like the ones found on the Internet to allow employees to discuss projects efficiently. Using video chat on an intranet makes it possible to hold meetings with people in another office or even a different building.

# INTRANET WEB SITES

**Sites on an intranet Web system are similar to Web sites found on the World Wide Web.**

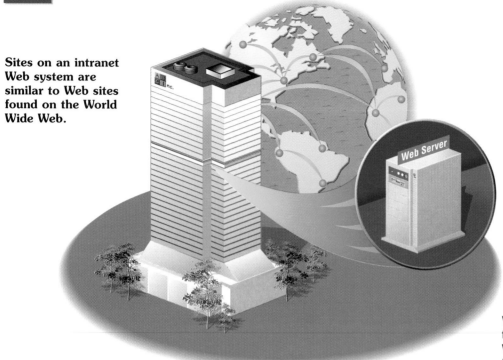

Web servers connected to a network store the Web sites and manage the intranet Web system.

## COMPATIBILITY

Intranets are very useful for companies that have different types of computers, such as IBM-compatible and Macintosh. Any computer that can run a Web browser can access the information available on an intranet Web site.

## SECURITY

Many companies that have an intranet are also connected to the Internet. Most companies use a computer dedicated to maintaining security on the intranet to prevent people on the Internet from accessing information on the intranet. If someone tries to access the intranet from anywhere outside the intranet, the security computer will alert the network administrator.

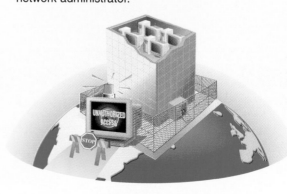

## EMPLOYEE WEB PAGES

If employees are connected to an intranet, they can easily publish their own Web pages. Web pages can contain information such as office telephone numbers, current projects or any other information that might be important to fellow employees.

## DEPARTMENT WEB PAGES

If a company has an intranet, any department in the company can display information on its own set of Web pages. For example, the human resources department may display company policies and schedules. The sales department might publish Web pages providing the latest sales figures.

## CREATE WEB PAGES

You can create a Web page for an intranet using the same software you would use to create a Web page for the World Wide Web. Most word processors, spreadsheets and database programs have a feature that makes it possible to save documents as Web pages. There are also many programs designed specifically for creating Web pages.

# INTRANET SOFTWARE

To set up an intranet, a company must have intranet software. There are many types of intranet software available.

## FREE SOFTWARE

Software available for the Internet, such as Web browsers, newsreaders and e-mail programs, can be used on a company's intranet. Many of these applications are available on the Internet free of charge.

## INTRANET SUITES

Most intranet software is available as a collection of several different applications sold together in one package, called a suite. Intranet suites usually consist of e-mail, Web publishing, database and security applications. When installing an intranet suite, you can decide which applications you want to use and install only those applications.

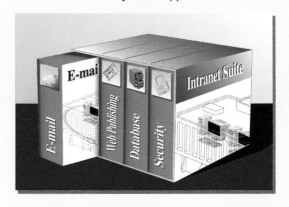

## POPULAR INTRANET SUITES

### MICROSOFT BACKOFFICE

Microsoft offers a set of intranet software called BackOffice. BackOffice includes popular intranet features, as well as an application that helps you easily organize and manage a large Web site. You can find information on BackOffice at the following Web site:

www.microsoft.com/backoffice

### NOVELL NETWARE FOR SMALL BUSINESS

NetWare for Small Business is a software suite offered by Novell. This suite includes applications that allow you to create databases and exchange network e-mail. You can find information on NetWare for Small Business at the following Web site:

www.novell.com/products/smallbiz/prodinfo.html

### LOTUS DOMINO

Lotus Domino, formerly known as Lotus Notes, is a popular intranet suite. Domino provides many applications that make it easy to communicate and share information on an intranet. You can find information on Domino at the following Web site:

www.lotus.com/domino

# INTRANET SECURITY

Many companies that have intranets are also connected to the Internet. You must take precautions when connecting any computer or network to the Internet.

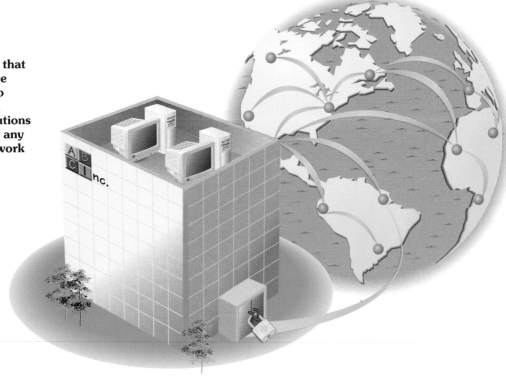

## FIREWALLS

A firewall is software or a computer that restricts the information that passes between a private intranet and the Internet. Many companies use a firewall to prevent unauthorized individuals from accessing the intranet.

## ACCESS RESTRICTIONS

Some companies restrict people on the intranet from accessing certain parts of the Internet, such as chat rooms. If a company restricts access to Web sites on the World Wide Web, employees will still be able to view information on the intranet Web site.

## PASSWORDS

Some intranet services, such as newsgroups, require you to enter a login name and password to view information. Login names and passwords ensure that unauthorized employees do not have access to confidential company information.

## OPERATING SYSTEM UPDATES

The operating system used on an intranet often has built-in security features to protect the information on the intranet. Operating systems are frequently updated to protect against the latest security concerns. The network administrator should ensure that the latest updates to the operating system are installed on each computer on the intranet.

## VIRUSES

A virus is a program that disrupts the normal operation of a computer. A virus can cause a variety of problems, such as the appearance of annoying messages on the screen or the destruction of information on the hard drive. Most companies frequently check for viruses on each computer connected to an intranet.

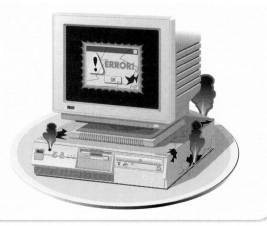

# DIGGING UP THE PAST
## A GUIDE TO ARCHAEOLOGICAL DIGS

*"We provide the most comprehensive, educational and informative resource on archaeological studies. Digging up the past to uncover the future."*

These pages contain descriptions of archaeological excavations in progress around the world. Professional archaeologists can use our pages to stay on top of the latest archaeological finds. Amateurs can research topics of interest and find out which digs accept volunteers.

The information is divided geographically into five regions: Africa, Asia, Europe, Oceania and The Americas. Within each region, you can select a country and browse through an extensive list of excavations. Or you can search for a specific dig by place name or key word.

**History**

# BIRD WATCHERS' HOME PAGE

*The page dedicated to people who love to watch birds!*

Bird watchers appreciate the beauty and wonder of birds and are always interested in ways to attract them. One of the best and easiest ways to draw birds to your backyard is to build a birdhouse. On this page, I will introduce you to steps you can follow to construct a simple birdhouse.

**STEP ONE: PREPARATION**

- Decide what type of bird you want to attract. This decision will influence the dimensions of the house and the size of the entry hole you must drill.
  - **SIZE CONSIDERATIONS**
- Purchase wood. Pine is my favorite choice, but other types of wood are fine.
- Make sure you have the necessary tools. You will need a saw, drill, hammer and nails.

**Animals**

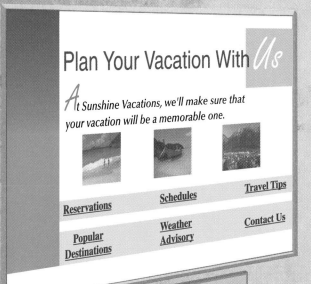

# Plan Your Vacation With *Us*

*A*t Sunshine Vacations, we'll make sure that your vacation will be a memorable one.

| | | |
|---|---|---|
| **Reservations** | **Schedules** | **Travel Tips** |
| **Popular Destinations** | **Weather Advisory** | **Contact Us** |

**Travel**

# Great Outdoor Trips
### • ADVENTURE TRIPS INC. •

- Fishing in Colorado
- Mountain Climbing in the Rockies
- White Water Rafting in Costa Rica

**Sports**

elcome
Web P

Computers:

## CHAPTER 14

# Interesting Web Sites

*Would you like to visit some great Web sites? This chapter includes a collection of interesting Web sites you can visit.*

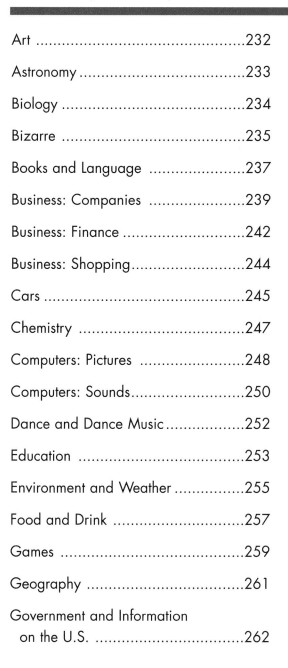

## ART

### ArtMecca

Portal to the art world! Search for works by your favorite artist or check out the links to some famous museums!

**URL** www.artmecca.com

### ArtQuest

Need something to spruce up the living room or fill that blank wall? Check out this site.

**URL** www.artquest.com

### ArtScape Gallery

Have an eye for art? Check out the work of some of the finest up-and-coming artists in the world at this extensive gallery.

**URL** artscapegallery.com

### Electric Gallery

This site offers many paintings that you can view and even buy if you like.

**URL** www.egallery.com

### Kspace

This site offers a wide variety of work from independent artists.

**URL** kspace.com

### Museum of Bad Art

The place for art too bad to be ignored.

**URL** www.glyphs.com/moba

### Museum of Modern Art

Peruse the extensive art collection displayed at this Web site and do some shopping from their online store while you're at it!

**URL** www.moma.org

### National Endowment for the Arts

Read all about art in the United States and view the art gallery at this detailed Web site.

**URL** arts.endow.gov

### National Museum of American Art

View almost 1,000 works of art from across the United States.

**URL** www.nmaa.si.edu

### Photo of the Day

See the world through a different perspective by visiting this Web site and checking out the photo of the day.

**URL** www.tssphoto.com/potd.html

## ASTRONOMY

### Bradford Robotic Telescope Observatory

This great guide to the universe is taken from a multimedia CD-ROM.

**URL** www.eia.brad.ac.uk/btl

### NASA

NASA presents pictures, information and links to all major NASA research locations in the U.S.

**URL** www.nasa.gov

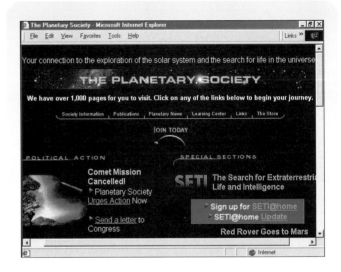

### NASA Human Spaceflight

NASA's status report keeps you up-to-date on the space shuttle.

**URL** shuttle.nasa.gov

### National Space Science Data Center

This site contains a photo gallery and various space-related information.

**URL** nssdc.gsfc.nasa.gov

### Planetary Society

Explore the solar system and search for life in the universe with this amazing site!

**URL** www.planetary.org

### Views of the Solar System

Travel light years away with the click of your mouse.

**URL** spaceart.com/solar

## BIOLOGY

### Bio Online
One of the top sites for information on biotechnology.
**URL** www.bio.com

### Biology Links
A guide to biology on the Internet.
**URL** mcb.harvard.edu/BioLinks.html

### Cell Online
A collection of biology journals.
**URL** www.cell.com

### Dictionary of Cell Biology
You can find those important definitions for your next biology essay.
**URL** www.mblab.gla.ac.uk/dictionary

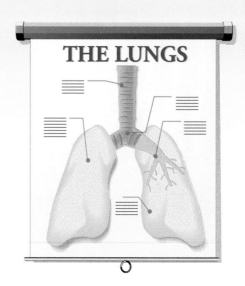

THE LUNGS

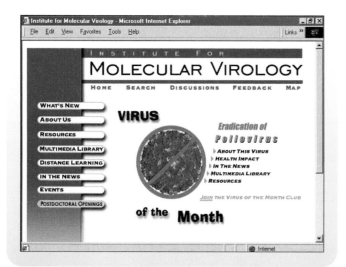

### Entomology
Colorado State's collection of bug information.
**URL** www.colostate.edu/Depts/Entomology

### Institute for Molecular Virology
Articles, pictures and information concerning various viruses.
**URL** www.bocklabs.wisc.edu/Welcome.html

### PharmInfoNet
If you want information on prescription drugs or on pharmacies in general, look here.
**URL** www.pharminfo.com

### USGS Biology
A directory of biological science sites on the Web.
**URL** info.er.usgs.gov/network/science/biology

## BIZARRE

### Anagram Fun

Give this Web page a phrase and it will use the letters to make another sentence.

**URL** www.anagramfun.com

### Bad Fads Museum

From bellbottoms to tie-dye t-shirts, step back in time and reminisce about the fads that have come and gone throughout the years.

**URL** www.badfads.com

### Bad Movie Night

Who says a movie has to be good to be enjoyable? This is a fun site where you can read or post reviews about the worst movies to come out of Hollywood!

**URL** www.hit-n-run.com

### Bizarre Links

Looking for some fun? This site provides links to the weird, bizarre, abnormal and mysterious sites!

**URL** www.logiko.com/links/bizarre.html

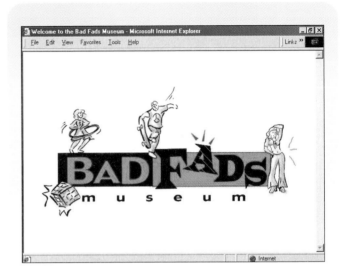

### Blue Dog

A dog will bark the correct answer to a math question you ask.

**URL** www.forbesfield.com/bdf.html

### Captain Kirk Sing-a-long Page

William Shatner croons his heart out on this quirky page.

**URL** www.loskene.com/singalong/kirk.html

### Center for the Easily Amused

Bored? Check out this Web site for hours of wacky fun and entertainment.

**URL** www.amused.com

### Coloring.com

Color a picture of anything from an apple to a leprechaun at this site.

**URL** www.coloring.com

### Contortion Home Page

A page dedicated to some very flexible individuals.

**URL** www.contortionhomepage.com

### Driveways of the Rich and Famous

See the driveways of your favorite stars! Also hear interviews from the people that know the stars the best—their gardeners and mailmen!

**URL** www.driveways.com

### International Museum of Toilets

This virtual toilet museum is where you will find everything you've ever wanted to know about toilets. And probably some things you didn't want to know!

**URL** www.sulabhtoiletmuseum.org

### Land O' Useless Facts

Get a daily dose of useless trivia or browse through the extensive archives of useless facts.

**URL** www.useless-facts.com

### Mr. Edible Starchy Tuber Head

An online toy that just happens to look like the Mr. Potatohead doll.

**URL** winnie.acsu.buffalo.edu/potatoe

### Optical Illusions

Let your eyes play tricks on you at this interesting Web site. There are 27 optical illusions that are bound to boggle your mind.

**URL** members.aol.com/Ryanbut/optical.html

### Send a Virtual Postcard

Send a postcard to someone else on the Internet via this site at MIT.

**URL** postcards.www.media.mit.edu/Postcards

### Toilet Paper Online

What this online magazine lacks in news, it makes up for in laughs.

**URL** www.thetp.com

### T.W.I.N.K.I.E.S.

Tests With Inorganic Noxious Kakes In Extreme Situations. That's right, you can watch Twinkies blow up into a million pieces.

**URL** www.owlnet.rice.edu/~gouge/twinkies.html

## BOOKS AND LANGUAGE

### Amazon.com

The popular Amazon.com offers more than 4.7 million titles at everyday sales of up to 40% off! Search their catalogs or browse for something new!

**URL** www.amazon.com

### AudioBooks

A catalog of books on tape.

**URL** www.audiobooks.com

### barnesandnoble.com

This site claims: "If we don't have your book, nobody does!" Their collection consists of bestsellers, recommended books and even out-of-print and rare books!

**URL** www.barnesandnoble.com

### Best Book Buys

Don't pay more than you have to! This site helps you compare prices for the book you want so you can get the best deal.

**URL** www.bestbookbuys.com

### Books@Random

One of North America's largest publishers. Find information on their books, a daily horoscope and more.

**URL** www.bdd.com

### Books.com

Looking for lively conversation on your favorite books and authors? Then visit this site and exercise your mind in discussion forums or find a book from almost any category!

**URL** www.books.com

### BookWire

A good place to start if you're looking for book information.

**URL** www.bookwire.com

## BOOKS AND LANGUAGE *continued*

### Children's Literature

A guide to books for the little ones. This site has databases, reviews and you can even meet the authors and illustrators!

**URL** www.childrenslit.com

### Elements of Style

Can't figure out where to place that comma in the sentence? Learn some common rules of the English language at this site.

**URL** www.columbia.edu/acis/bartleby/strunk

### English Server

Carnegie Mellon University uses this site to distribute research, novels, criticism and much more.

**URL** english-www.hss.cmu.edu

### IDG Books

IDG publishes the Dummies series, the 3-D Visual series and many others.

**URL** www.idgbooks.com

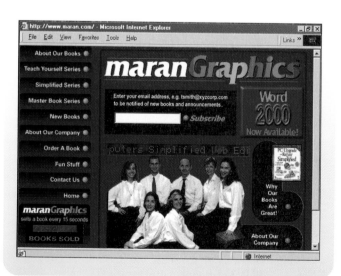

### Internet Public Library

A reference library at the click of a button!

**URL** www.ipl.org

### Library of Congress

You can't read the books online, but you can search for one of interest.

**URL** lcweb.loc.gov

### maranGraphics

Find out more about the world's most user-friendly computer books.

**URL** www.maran.com

### On-line Books

A collection of books at Carnegie Mellon University.

**URL** www.cs.cmu.edu/Web/books.html

### Virtual Reference Desk

Use a thesaurus, dictionary or phone book here.

**URL** thorplus.lib.purdue.edu/reference

## BUSINESS: COMPANIES

### 7-Eleven

Go behind the scenes to find out what's new at your local convenience store.

**URL** www.seveneleven.com

### AT&T

This site offers a wide variety of telecommunications services.

**URL** www.att.com

### Best Western International

At this site you can view hotel information and make reservations online at any Best Western hotel in the world.

**URL** www.bestwestern.com

### Crayola

This site tells you how crayons are made and allows you to color online.

**URL** www.crayola.com

### FAO Schwarz

More toys than you can imagine.

**URL** www.faoschwarz.com

### FedEx

Track your package online and make sure it arrives safely.

**URL** www.fedex.com

### GTE Internet

GTE gives you access to information and resources on the Internet. Send e-mail, surf the Net, visit chat rooms or join newsgroups.

**URL** www.gte.net

**BUSINESS: COMPANIES** *continued*

### Guess

Go behind the scenes at a Guess photo-shoot or send a digital postcard to a friend.

**URL** www.guess.com

### JCPenney

This chain of department stores lets you browse through their products from the comfort of your own home.

**URL** www.jcpenney.com

### Joe Boxer

This site is less about underwear and more about having fun!

**URL** www.joeboxer.com

### Kodak

This site offers a great collection of digital images.

**URL** www.kodak.com

### Labatt

Information on Labatt and its products.

**URL** www.labattblue.com

### Milk

Do you have a thirst for knowledge? Then moo-ve to this site to learn all about milk. From recipes and nutritional information, to photos of celebrities sporting the famous milk mustache, this site will quench your curiosity!

**URL** www.whymilk.com

### Neiman Marcus

Get the latest news from the fashion world or find out what is happening at Neiman Marcus this month.

**URL** www.neimanmarcus.com

### Pepsi

Hang around Pepsi World and win fabulous prizes!

**URL** www.pepsi.com

### Philips

This huge electronics company showcases its products and company information.

**URL** www.philips.com

### Ragu

This is a top-notch site with recipes, contests and guides to speaking Italian.

**URL** www.eat.com

### Sprint

Find out all about the long distance company at this site.

**URL** www.sprint.com

### Sunkist

Squeeze some fresh fun into your day by visiting this Web site, which features games, recipes and more!

**URL** www.sunkist.com

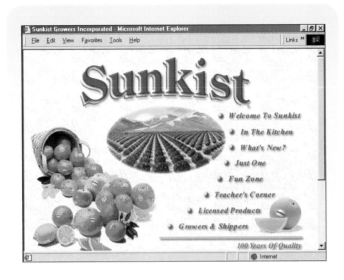

### Ticketmaster

Look up events, read interviews and win free concert tickets!

**URL** U.S. www.ticketmaster.com
**URL** Canada www.ticketmaster.ca

### UPS

Use the United Parcel Service site to track your package across the country.

**URL** www.ups.com

### Virtual Vineyards

From fine wines to delectable hors d'oeuvres, you'll find it all at Virtual Vineyards.

**URL** www.virtualvin.com

### Wal-Mart

Shop for bargains at this Web site.

**URL** www.wal-mart.com

## BUSINESS: FINANCE

### American Stock Exchange

Check today's market summary or look back through the archives for the past year.

**URL** www.amex.com

### bankonline.com

An online banking and financial services directory.

**URL** www.bankonline.com

### Citibank

One of the largest banks in the U.S.

**URL** www.citicorp.com

### Coin Universe

Resources for collectors, dealers and anyone else interested in coins from around the world.

**URL** www.coin-universe.com

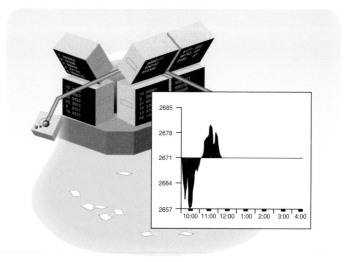

### Electronic Banker

An information-packed resource for people who do their banking through the Internet.

**URL** www.electronicbanker.com

### Finance on the WWW

This site in Denmark is filled with links to business and finance.

**URL** www.wiso.gwdg.de/ifbg/finance.html

### Investor's Business Daily

Be one of over 800,000 people who check out this online newspaper each day for the latest in business news.

**URL** www.investors.com

### Money

A great source of financial information, from loan rates to investment ideas.

**URL** www.pathfinder.com/money

## Mutual Funds Interactive

Get advice from the experts before you part with your hard-earned cash.

**URL** www.brill.com

## PCQuote

A great place to get delayed stock quotes free of charge.

**URL** www.pcquote.com

## Principal Financial Group

The place to look for information on retirement plans, mutual funds, life insurance and many other investment ideas.

**URL** www.principal.com

## StockMaster

Check out which stocks and mutual funds are hot.

**URL** www.stockmaster.com

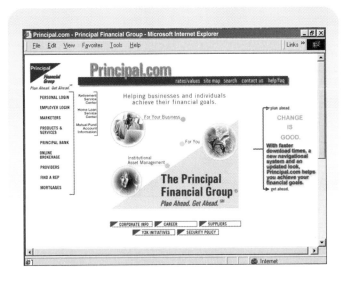

## USA Today - Money

Read about what's new in the financial world.

**URL** www.usatoday.com/money

## Wells Fargo

The oldest bank in the West has a wide variety of services on the Internet.

**URL** www.wellsfargo.com

## World Bank Group

Find out all about the World Bank at this site.

**URL** www.worldbank.org

## WSJ

The Wall Street Journal's business news page.

**URL** update.wsj.com

# BC

## BUSINESS: SHOPPING

### Access Market Square

You can find many unique products and gifts at this site.

**URL** www.icw.com/ams.html

### BrandsForLess

Looking for name brands at big discounts? Visit BrandsForLess and shop their e-partments!

**URL** www.brandsforless.com

### Catalog Mart

The easiest and fastest way to get just about any catalog available in the U.S. Choose from more than 10,000—all free!

**URL** catalog.savvy.com

### Columbia House

Build a collection of CDs, DVDs or movies by joining Columbia House. Browse through thousands of titles at this Web site!

**URL** www.columbiahouse.com

### eBay

Going once, going twice...Don't let that great deal get away! Bid on all kinds of items at this auction Web site.

**URL** www.ebay.com

### eMall

Products, services and information— this site has something for everyone.

**URL** www.eMall.com

### Fingerhut Online

Fingerhut offers a wide variety of products including jewelry, electronics, clothing and much more.

**URL** www.fingerhut.com

### iMALL

Check out the deals of the day, browse iMALL's classifieds or search for an item of interest at this Web site.

**URL** www.imall.com

### Internet Shopping Network

A site with hot deals and Internet specials.

**URL** www.internet.net

### NECX

Millions of computer products are available here.

**URL** www.necx.com

### Shop at Home

Search by name, keyword or category for a catalog of interest.

**URL** www.shopathome.com

### ShopNow.com

Find out where you can purchase food, clothing, furniture, gifts and much more.

**URL** www.internet-mall.com

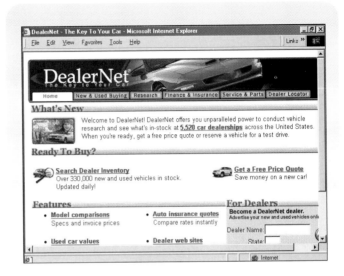

ARS

### Alamo

Reserve a car online and check out the weather for where you are headed.

**URL** www.freeways.com

### Autoweb.com

Advertised as "The Internet's Premier Auto Mall."

**URL** www.autoweb.com

### Cadillac

You can find information on the new Cadillacs or check out upcoming Cadillac-sponsored events.

**URL** www.cadillac.com

### DealerNet

A great consumer resource for new and used vehicle buying information.

**URL** www.dealernet.com

### Ford Motor Company

All the Ford information your heart desires.

**URL** www.ford.com

### General Motors

A comprehensive site from the world's largest car maker.

**URL** www.gm.com

### Goodyear

They've got lots of tires and a very big blimp.

**URL** www.goodyear.com

### Harley Davidson Motorcycles of Stamford

Okay, so it's not a car—it still has wheels.

**URL** www.hd-stamford.com

### Honda

Honda in America features a dealer locator, owner information, new model updates and more.

**URL** www.honda.com

### Jeep

For those who crave the rugged outdoors.

**URL** www.jeepunpaved.com

### Nissan

Visit the Nissan site and go on the Nissan Journey.

**URL** www.nissandriven.com

### Saturn

This site is geared towards Saturn owners, but prospective buyers should also check it out.

**URL** www.saturncars.com

### Toyota

You can find information on Toyota's vehicles, dealers and much more.

**URL** www.toyota.com

### Volvo

Check out the new line of Volvos or locate the dealer nearest you.

**URL** www.volvocars.com

## CHEMISTRY

### Chemie.de Information Service

Information on chemistry software, conferences, jobs and more.

**URL** www.chemie.de

### Chemistry

This site provides links to chemistry departments around the world.

**URL** www.chem.ucla.edu/
chempointers.html

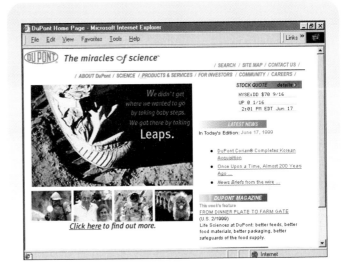

### Chemistry Hypermedia Project

Provides resources and educational material for chemistry students.

**URL** www.chem.vt.edu/chem-ed/
vt-chem-ed.html

### Chemist's Art Gallery

Pictures and animations of molecules and other aspects of chemistry.

**URL** www.csc.fi/lul/chem/graphics.html

### DuPont

Check out one of the largest science companies!

**URL** www.dupont.com

### Ethics in Science

Includes the Chemist's Code of Conduct, and essays about the rights and wrongs of science in general.

**URL** www.chem.vt.edu/ethics/ethics.html

CHEMISTRY *continued*

### Internet Journal of Chemistry
The electronic journal for chemists!
**URL** www.ijc.com

### National Academy of Sciences
A list of scientific committees and resources across the U.S.
**URL** www4.nas.edu/nas/nashome.nsf

### Periodic Table of the Elements
Click on an element in the Periodic Table to get information about that element.
**URL** pearl1.lanl.gov/periodic

### Royal Society of Chemistry
This site is for students, teachers or anyone interested in chemistry.
**URL** chemistry.rsc.org/rsc

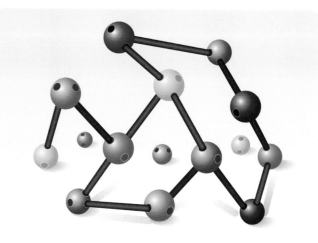

### Wilson-Squier Group
This chemistry research site will help you visualize molecules.
**URL** www-wilson.ucsd.edu

## COMPUTERS: PICTURES

### Animation Library
From dancing elephants to sailboats, this site features over 3,500 fun animations you can use for free.
**URL** www.animationlibrary.com

### Clip Art Connection
Thousands of free clip art images you can use.
**URL** www.clipartconnection.com

### Cool Science Images
Lots of incredibly cool pictures of insects, viruses, planets and more.
**URL** whyfiles.news.wisc.edu/ coolimages

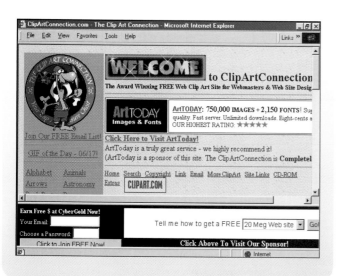

### John Donohue's National Park Photos

Excellent photos of America's best national parks.

**URL** www.panix.com/~wizjd/parks/parks.html

### Kite Aerial Photography

Want a new perspective? Check out these pictures taken from a camera attached to a kite.

**URL** www-archfp.ced.berkeley.edu/kap

### Lighthouses

Pictures of lighthouses from around the world.

**URL** www.ipl.org/exhibit/light

### Michigan Press Photographer's Association

Browse through the winning photos in the Pictures of the Year contest.

**URL** www.mppa.org

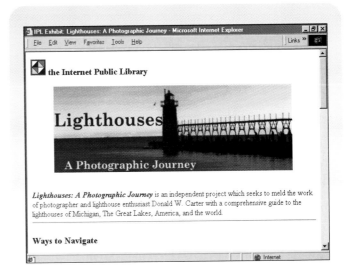

### Microsoft© Clip Gallery Live

You can easily find clip art at this site! Simply type in a keyword or search by category to find clips related to a particular topic. New clips are added every month!

**URL** www.microsoft.com/clipgallerylive

### NSSDC Photo Gallery

The National Space Science Data Center has pictures of planets, asteroids and more.

**URL** nssdc.gsfc.nasa.gov/photo_gallery

### Photo Exhibitions and Archives

A list of photo exhibits on the Web.

**URL** www.algonet.se/~bengtha/photo/exhibits.html

### SunSite Archive

A huge list of pictures sorted into categories.

**URL** sunsite.unc.edu/pub/multimedia/pictures

## COMPUTERS: SOUNDS

### 60 Second Theatre
Audio dramas under a minute in length can be found here. Dozens of plays are available for you to listen to.
**URL** www.letusout.com

### Creative
Makers of the popular Sound Blaster sound card.
**URL** www.creaf.com

### Guide to Animal Sounds on the Net
Go wild in this site with links to animal sounds from frogs to whales.
**URL** members.tripod.com/Thryomanes/
AnimalSounds.html

### Historic Audio Archives
Listen to speeches by Richard Nixon, JFK and many others.
**URL** www.webcorp.com/sounds/
index.htm

### Internet Underground Music Archive
A cool place to hear independent artists and bands.
**URL** www.iuma.com

### Japanese Sound Archive
The sounds have nothing to do with Japan, but this site is large and fast.
**URL** sunsite.sut.ac.jp/multimed/sounds

### Metalab Sounds
You can find songs, quotes and more in this large sound collection.
**URL** metalab.unc.edu/pub/multimedia/
pc-sounds

### Movie Sounds
Sounds from all of your favorite movies.
**URL** www.moviesounds.com

### mp3.com

Find out how to collect high quality mp3 music recordings and download the songs of your choice!

**URL** www.mp3.com

### RealNetworks®

Download the RealPlayer® software to easily listen to sounds and view movies on your computer.

**URL** www.real.com

### Sound of the Day

Each day a new sound can be found here. Listen to the song of the day or select one from the extensive archives!

**URL** web-star.com/sod/sod.html

### SoundAmerica

Having trouble finding a specific sound? Try SoundAmerica. They have over 26,300 sounds available on this Web site.

**URL** www.soundamerica.com

### Text to Speech

Type something and this Web site will actually say it back!

**URL** wwwtios.cs.utwente.nl/say

### The Answering Machine

Surprise callers by downloading an answering machine message from this unique Web site. Includes messages from famous movies, songs and personalities.

**URL** www.answeringmachine.co.uk

### Vincent Voice Library

A selection of historical speeches and lectures.

**URL** www.lib.msu.edu/vincent/

### Warsaw University

Warsaw is one of many universities around the world that have collections of sound.

**URL** info.fuw.edu.pl/multimedia/sounds

## DANCE AND DANCE MUSIC

### Any Swing Goes

Swing by this site for the latest news and music or to chat with other swing enthusiasts.

**URL** www.anyswinggoes.com

### CyberDance-Ballet on the Net

A great source for links to ballet and modern dance information on the Internet.

**URL** www.thepoint.net/~raw/dance.htm

### Dance Online

You will find information on performances, reviews and links to other Web sites.

**URL** www.danceonline.com

### DanceArt.com

This site is jam-packed with great information to help you ace that audition, improve your technique, or find the right dance gear.

**URL** www.danceart.com

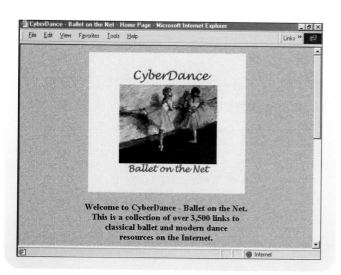

### DancerOnline

An online version of the popular dance magazine, this site offers news, features, links and much more.

**URL** www.danceronline.com

### Dancescape

Wanna tango? Take a quick step into the world of competitive ballroom dancing and learn how it's done.

**URL** www.dancescape.com

### Ernesto's Tango Page

Put a rose between your teeth before you visit this site.

**URL** members.ping.at/kdf-wien/tango

### Gaynor Minden

Are your pointe shoes ill-fitting or uncomfortable? If the shoe doesn't fit, you'll want to visit this site of one of the world's leading dance shoe makers.

**URL** www.dancer.com

## Information Super Dance Floor

A great resource for those who want to learn the latest country music dance steps.

**URL** www.apci.net/~drdeyne

## New York City Ballet

Find out when and where this world-renowned ballet company will be performing.

**URL** www.nycballet.com

## Sapphire Swan Dance Directory

Whatever your beat, you can find links to great sites from this spot.

**URL** www.sapphireswan.com/dance

## Streetsound

A site designed for dance music DJs and fans.

**URL** www.streetsound.com

## Tap Dance Homepage

This site's extensive collection of tap dancing links is definitely something to tap about.

**URL** www.tapdance.org

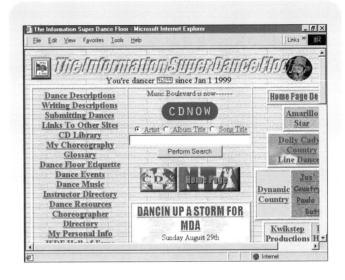

## The Dance Shop

Browse this extensive catalog to get all the supplies you need for practice or for that special performance.

**URL** www.dancers4dancers.com

# EDUCATION

## AskERIC

This service is well-known for its resources for teachers.

**URL** ericir.syr.edu

## CollegeNET

A searchable database of over 2,000 universities and colleges.

**URL** www.collegenet.com

### EdLinks

Links to educational sites of every size and shape.

**URL** webpages.marshall.edu/~jmullens/
edlinks.html

### Education Index

Whether you're an exceptional scholar or a struggling student, this index provides you with links to fascinating educational Web sites.

**URL** www.educationindex.com

### fastWEB

A guide to finding university and college scholarships.

**URL** www.studentservices.com/fastweb

### Frank Potter's Science Gems

A collection of science and mathematics resources available on the Web.

**URL** www-sci.lib.uci.edu/SEP/SEP.html

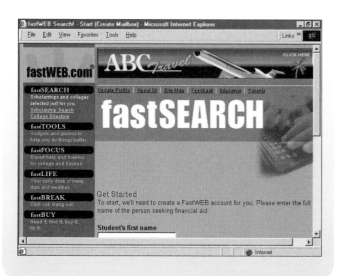

### Global Schoolhouse

This site is dedicated to linking kids around the world, offering projects, contests and much more.

**URL** www.globalschoolhouse.org

### Global Show-n-Tell

Kids can show their stuff to other kids around the world.

**URL** www.telenaut.com/gst

### Kidlink

This site offers several different forums that allow 10 to 15-year-old students around the world to communicate.

**URL** www.kidlink.org

### KidPub

Where kids and classes can post their stories and poems.

**URL** www.kidpub.org

### Kids' Space

A fantastic place for kids to share their imaginations with other kids.

**URL** www.kids-space.org

### Media Literacy Online Project

A collection of information about the influence of the media in the lives of children.

**URL** interact.uoregon.edu/MediaLit/
HomePage

### Online Educational Resources

A collection of educational resources for students and teachers.

**URL** quest.arc.nasa.gov/OER

### Teaching and Learning on the Web

From courses delivered on the Web to class projects, find examples of how others are using the Web as a learning tool.

**URL** www.mcli.dist.maricopa.edu/tl

### Yale University

Find out about programs and campus life at Yale.

**URL** www.yale.edu

## ENVIRONMENT AND WEATHER

### Department of Atmospheric Sciences

This site has links to several weather resources on the World Wide Web.

**URL** www.atmos.uiuc.edu

### Earth Force

Find out what young people in communities across the United States are doing to protect the environment and promote conservation awareness.

**URL** www.earthforce.org

### EcoNet

EcoNet has several sister networks, including PeaceNet, LaborNet and WomensNet.

**URL** www.igc.apc.org/econet

### EnviroLink Network

One of the world's largest sources of online environmental information.

**URL** www.envirolink.org

### Environmental Protection Agency

Learn how the government is making a difference.

**URL** www.epa.gov

### Greenpeace

While you can't race alongside an oil tanker online, this WWW site gives you a taste of Greenpeace.

**URL** www.greenpeace.org

### Intellicast

Check out the weather around the world.

**URL** www.intellicast.com

### National Oceanic and Atmospheric Administration

Find out what the U.S. government is doing about the ozone layer, endangered species and more.

**URL** www.noaa.gov

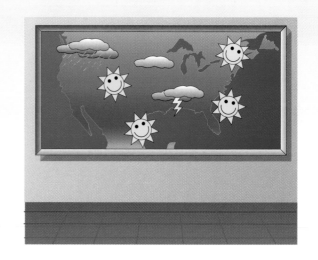

### Rainforest Action Network

This site promotes the preservation of the Earth's rainforests.

**URL** www.ran.org

### Recycler's World

A site dedicated to recycling.

**URL** www.recycle.net

### USA Today Weather

Weather information from one of the largest newspapers in the U.S.

**URL** www.usatoday.com/weather

### Water Science for Schools

Water, water, everywhere—water actually covers two-thirds of the earth's surface! Find out about water cycles, properties, and how we use this valuable resource.

**URL** ga.water.usgs.gov/edu

### Weather Information Superhighway

This site offers links to many weather-related Web pages.

**URL** www.nws.fsu.edu/wxhwy.html

### WeatherNet: Weather Cams

Spy on the weather with current pictures taken from cameras mounted all over the U.S. and Canada.

**URL** cirrus.sprl.umich.edu/wxnet/wxcam.html

# FOOD AND DRINK

### Ask the Dietitian

Low in fat. High in fiber. What does it all mean? Ask the Dietitian.

**URL** www.dietitian.com

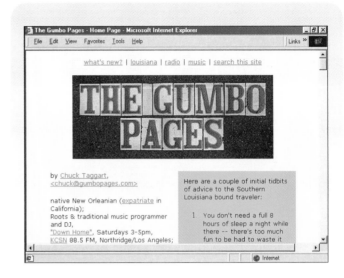

### Coca-Cola

This site has information on the company and its products, as well as little things to amuse you.

**URL** www.cocacola.com

### Godiva Chocolates

This site includes recipes and the chance to shop for all your chocolate needs online.

**URL** www.godiva.com

### Gumbo Pages

You can find information on the food, music and culture of New Orleans.

**URL** www.gumbopages.com

### Hershey Foods Corporation

The company known for its chocolate kisses.

**URL** www.hersheys.com

### Ketchum Kitchen

See what's cooking in the Ketchum Kitchen. Recipes, discussions and much more are available here.

**URL** www.recipe.com

### Mentos

Find out what's new at the freshmaker's site or check out their live music concerts.

**URL** www.mentos.com

### Pasta Home Page

Pasta lovers, this is your site! Find recipes, answers to popular questions and information on nutrition and pasta shapes.

**URL** www.ilovepasta.org

### Perrier

This refreshing Web site has contests, a gallery of art bottles and much more.

**URL** www.perrier.com

### Recipe Archive

Learn to make everything from lasagna to cheesecake at this site.

**URL** www.cs.cmu.edu/~mjw/recipes

### Rubbermaid

Find information on the products that keep your food fresh!

**URL** www.rubbermaid.com

### StarChefs

Get recipes and tips from great chefs and cookbook authors.

**URL** www.starchefs.com

### Vegetarian Pages

News, recipes, a list of famous vegetarians and much more.

**URL** www.veg.org/veg

# GAMES

### Chess.net

Learn the game and compete with chess players from around the world at this Web site.

**URL** www.chess.net

### Electronic Arts

One of the top game-makers in North America.

**URL** www.ea.com

### Games Domain

This popular site offers free games and tips on some of the most popular computer games on the market.

**URL** www.gamesdomain.com

### Gamesmania

This comprehensive gaming Web site offers all kinds of information and tips on popular games. It even teaches you how to cheat!

**URL** www.gamesmania.com

### Happy Puppy

A huge collection of games, demos, strategy tips and more.

**URL** www.happypuppy.com

### Jumbo

A collection of free games and programs you can download.

**URL** www.jumbo.com

### LucasArts

Creators of many top-rated computer games.

**URL** www.lucasarts.com

### Need for Speed

Race your dream car on a variety of realistic courses. You can race against another player or choose to be a police officer in hot pursuit.

**URL** www.needforspeed.com

### Nintendo Power Source

Check out all the latest games. The fun never ends at this Web site!

**URL** www.nintendo.com

### PC Gamer Online

Find reviews, previews and gaming news at the online outpost of this computer gaming magazine.

**URL** www.pcgamer.com

### Riddler

Solve puzzles and riddles for cash and prizes.

**URL** www.riddler.com

### Sega Online

Find out more about the games this video game giant offers.

**URL** www.sega.com

### Shareware.com

This powerful tool helps you find programs that you can copy to your computer.

**URL** www.shareware.com

### Virtual Stock Exchange

Ever dream of being a high profile stock trader? Now you can enjoy all the thrills without the risk with this virtual stock market game.

**URL** crosswalk.virtualstockexchange.com

### Virtual Vegas

Virtual Vegas has blackjack, poker, roulette and more for the gambler in you.

**URL** www.virtualvegas.com

### Where's Waldo? on the Web!

Based on the popular Where's Waldo books, this Web site will have you searching for Waldo for hours!

**URL** www.findwaldo.com

# GEOGRAPHY

### Association of American Geographers

Visit this site to learn how to get into the exciting field of geography.

**URL** www.geography.org

### How far is it?

Enter two places and this Web site will tell you the distance between them.

**URL** www.indo.com/distance

### Mt. Rushmore

Don't you wish your face was up there too?

**URL** www.state.sd.us./tourism/rushmore

### National Climatic Data Center

Find out where it's hot and where it's not.

**URL** www.ncdc.noaa.gov

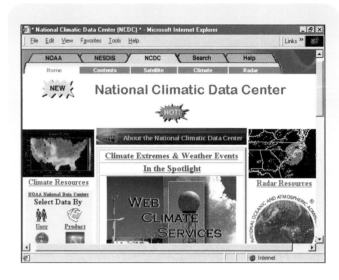

### National Geographic

Travel the world with National Geographic's renowned writers and photographers at this Web site.

**URL** www.nationalgeographic.com

### NCGIA

Find out about the National Center for Geographic Information and Analysis.

**URL** www.ncgia.ucsb.edu

### PCL Map Collection

The mother of all map collections.

**URL** www.lib.utexas.edu/Libs/PCL/
Map_collection

### U.S. Geological Survey

This site provides information to help you better understand earth sciences.

**URL** www.usgs.gov

## GOVERNMENT AND INFORMATION ON THE U.S.

### Army
You can flip through Soldiers, an online magazine, visit other army-related sites and much more.
**URL** www.army.mil

### Census Bureau
Find out how many people are currently living in the U.S.
**URL** www.census.gov

### CIA
This is a public site, so you won't find the government's deepest, darkest secrets here.
**URL** www.odci.gov/cia

### Coast Guard
This isn't Baywatch!
**URL** www.uscg.mil

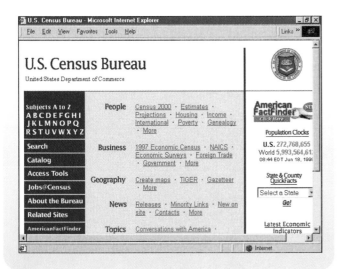

### DefenseLINK
The U.S. Defense Department's online handbook.
**URL** www.defenselink.mil

### Department of Education
This site provides information for both students and teachers.
**URL** www.ed.gov

### Department of Justice
They fight to protect your rights. This site has links to many agencies, including the FBI.
**URL** www.usdoj.gov

### FBI
Find out about the FBI and keep up-to-date on the latest investigations.
**URL** www.fbi.gov

## Federal Judiciary

A great source for information regarding the judicial branch of the U.S. government.

**URL** www.uscourts.gov

## FedStats

Do you have an inquiring mind? This site provides statistics and information from more than 70 federal government agencies.

**URL** www.fedstats.gov

## House of Representatives

This site provides information on legislation, committees and organizations of the House.

**URL** www.house.gov

## IBERT

Find out where all your money is going.

**URL** www.ibert.org

## IRS

Immediate access to the Internal Revenue Service tax information and services.

**URL** www.irs.gov

## Navy

All aboard! The complete guide to the U.S. Navy.

**URL** www.navy.mil

## New York State

The Empire State goes online!

**URL** www.state.ny.us

## Patent and Trademark Office

Find out about protecting your ideas with a patent or trademark. You can also search the Web Patent Database, which contains all the patents granted since 1976.

**URL** www.uspto.gov

## Postal Service

Look up a zip code, find a postage rate and much more here.

**URL** www.usps.gov

## Thomas Library

This immense site has a great deal of congressional and legislative information.

**URL** thomas.loc.gov

## Treasury Department

The people who make all our coins. This site provides information on the programs and activities of the U.S. Treasury Department.

**URL** www.ustreas.gov

## White House

See the First Family or take a tour of the White House.

**URL** www.whitehouse.gov

Australia     United Kingdom     Saudi Arabia

# GOVERNMENTS AND INFORMATION ON THE WORLD

## Australian Government

Information on the government of the Land Down Under.

**URL** www.fed.gov.au

## Europa Home Page

This site offers information on the European Union's goals and policies.

**URL** europa.eu.int

## Government of Canada

Get the facts about Canada's government, political structure and services.

**URL** www.canada.gc.ca

## Hong Kong Government Information Center

Pictures, government offices, news updates and a lot more on Hong Kong.

**URL** www.info.gov.hk

## International Foundation for Election Systems

This Web site offers loads of information about elections around the world. Find out who's voting when and follow the latest election news.

**URL** www.ifes.org

## New Zealand

Learn all there is to know about this country in the Pacific.

**URL** www.govt.nz

## Russia Today

Take a look at what is happening in Russia today with this site's thorough coverage of Russian politics.

**URL** www.russiatoday.com

## South African Government Information

Visit this site to learn more about South Africa.

**URL** www.polity.org.za

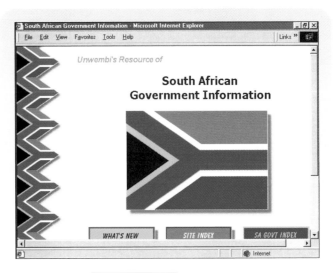

## United Kingdom

This site helps you locate government offices, services and officials in the United Kingdom.

**URL** www.open.gov.uk

## United Nations

Take a tour of the U.N. or keep up-to-date with the latest information on international relations.

**URL** www.un.org

# HEALTH

## Acupuncture.com

If you don't like needles, point your Web browser in another direction.

**URL** www.acupuncture.com

## American Medical Association

You can find medical journals and much more at this site.

**URL** www.ama-assn.org

### Centers for Disease Control

Learn how to prevent and control many diseases, injuries and disabilities.

**URL** www.cdc.gov

### Central Institute for the Deaf

This site provides information on the Institute's programs and education for the hearing impaired.

**URL** www.cid.wustl.edu

### Cyber Pharmacy

Do you have diabetes? Suffering from hair loss? Would you like to quit smoking? Visit this site and have all your questions answered from an experienced pharmacist! Patients can also order medication and refill prescriptions quickly and easily.

**URL** www.cyberpharmacy.com

### Eli Lilly and Company

Find out about treatments for diseases such as cancer and diabetes.

**URL** www.lilly.com

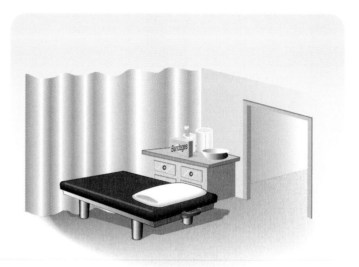

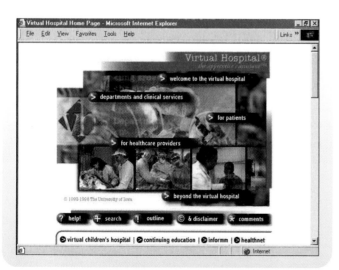

### Medical Breakthroughs

Be informed with the up-to-date medical news at this site.

**URL** www.ivanhoe.com

### National Library of Medicine

Access medical and scientific information from this huge library.

**URL** www.nlm.nih.gov

### Virtual Hospital

Find the latest health information at this Web site.

**URL** www.vh.org

### Virtual Medical Center

A large collection of medical information, as well as glossaries and dictionaries.

**URL** www-sci.lib.uci.edu/HSG/Medical.html

# HISTORY

### 1492: An Ongoing Voyage

This exhibit examines how the discovery of America affected nations around the world.

**URL** metalab.unc.edu/expo/1492.exhibit/Intro.html

### American Memory

This glorious site will keep an American history buff busy for days.

**URL** rs6.loc.gov/amhome.html

### Colonial Williamsburg

Step back in time and visit the world's largest outdoor living history complex, where the past comes to life!

**URL** www.history.org

### Encyclopedia.com

Researching a history topic? This is a great place to start!

**URL** www.encyclopedia.com

### Genealogy Home Page

A good starting point to trace your family tree.

**URL** www.genhomepage.com

### Greek Mythology

Greek Gods, heroes and The Odyssey! Check them all out at this site!

**URL** www.mythweb.com

### This Day in History

Learn what famous and not-so-famous events happened on this day in history.

**URL** www.historychannel.com/today

### U.S. Civil War Center

Learn more about the battle between the North and South.

**URL** www.cwc.lsu.edu

# HUMOR

### April Fools

A wide assortment of pranks for April Fool's Day, or any other day you feel mischievous!

**URL** aprilfools.infospace.com

### Ask Dr. Science

Check out Dr. Science's answer to the question of the day, ask him your own question or venture into his store to buy some wacky merchandise.

**URL** www.drscience.com

### Comedy Central

The all-comedy television network has a wacky site on the Web.

**URL** www.comcentral.com

### Ha!

Need a good laugh to brighten up your day? Have a joke to share? This site gives you the opportunity to do both!

**URL** www.hardyharhar.com

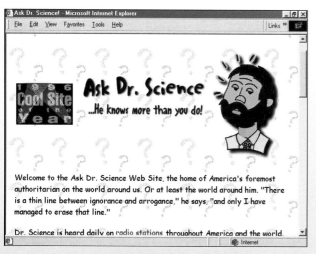

### Humor.com

Whether you're looking for hilarious jokes or zany news stories, you'll find a good laugh here.

**URL** www.humor.com

### Late Show Top 10 Archive

A collection of David Letterman's top ten lists.

**URL** marketing.cbs.com/lateshow/topten

### Laughter - The World's Common Language

This site finds humor in public speaking, social climbing, hosting a party and more!

**URL** www.laughter.com

### Rec.Humor.Funny Home Page

Thousands of jokes and humorous stories make this site a popular hangout for cyber-comedians.

**URL** comedy.clari.net/rhf

# J OBS

## America's Job Bank

There are thousands of jobs posted here by employment offices across the country.

**URL** www.ajb.dni.us

## Career.com

This site connects employers and job seekers around the world. A unique feature of career.com is the Virtual Job Fair.

**URL** www.career.com

## CareerMosaic

A collection of job postings from around the world.

**URL** www.careermosaic.com

## Employment Guide's CareerWEB

Find jobs from around the world, evaluate yourself with the Career Inventory or search the bookstore for job-related titles.

**URL** www.cweb.com

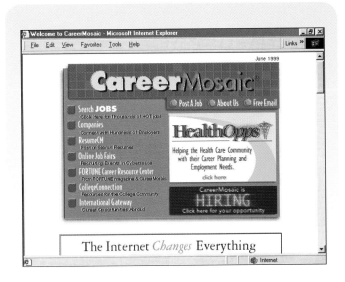

## Job-Hunt

A list of online employment resources.

**URL** www.job-hunt.org

## JobOptions

Opportunity knocks! This site could help open the door to a great new position.

**URL** www.joboptions.com

## Monster.com

The largest job search site on the Web! This monster site contains over 200,000 job openings and more than a million resumes for employers to search through.

**URL** www.monster.com

## NetJobs

Add a job or look one up.

**URL** www.netjobs.com

## MAGAZINES

### BusinessWeek Online
This online magazine will keep you informed about all the latest technology and business news!

**URL** www.businessweek.com

### Cosmopolitan
Check out this popular fashion magazine online!

**URL** www.cosmomag.com

### Enews.com
This electronic newsstand offers low subscription prices for magazine favorites such as Vogue, Newsweek and Forbes.

**URL** www.enews.com

### HotWired
The online edition of "Wired," the magazine dedicated to media, technology and pop culture.

**URL** www.hotwired.com

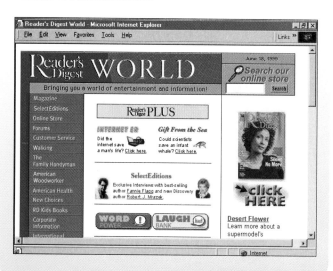

### Internet World
Check out this site and find out what's hot and what's not, on the Net!

**URL** www.iw.com

### OnTap
A hip look at entertainment, culture, sports and technology.

**URL** www.taponline.com

### Reader's Digest World
Visit this site for both entertainment and information!

**URL** www.readersdigest.com

### Salon
The magazine where politics and entertainment meet.

**URL** www.salon1999.com

### The Etext Archives

You can find many electronic magazines at this site.

**URL** www.etext.org/zines

### Time

This site includes excerpts from Time magazine.

**URL** www.time.com

### Word

This electronic magazine covers a variety of issues and includes stories, graphics and animation.

**URL** www.word.com

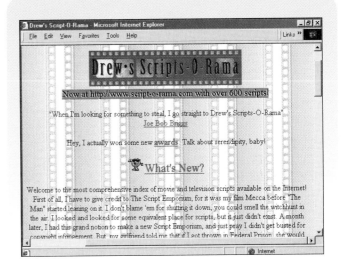

## MOVIES

### 007

This site is dedicated to James Bond.

**URL** www.mcs.net/~klast/www/bond.html

### Academy of Motion Picture Arts and Sciences

"And the Oscar goes to..." Visit this site to find out everything you ever wanted to know about the most popular entertainment awards.

**URL** www.oscars.org

### Alfred Hitchcock

Fans of "The Birds," "Vertigo" and "Psycho" should check out this site.

**URL** nextdch.mty.itesm.mx/~plopezg/
Kaplan/Hitchcock.html

### BigFellaMovies.com

Looking for humorous reviews of today's movies? Then check out this fun site!

**URL** www.bigfellamovies.com

### Drew's Scripts-O-Rama

You can look at more than 600 complete movie and T.V. scripts at this site.

**URL** www.script-o-rama.com

### Early Motion Pictures 1897-1920

A collection of some of the earliest films made in North America.

**URL** lcweb2.loc.gov/ammem/papr

### Film.com

This site includes reviews of most major movies and videos.

**URL** www.film.com

### FilmZone

A great magazine with lots of informative articles on independent, foreign, animated and Hollywood films.

**URL** www.filmzone.com

### Hollywood.com

A great source for information on the hottest movies and movie stars.

**URL** www.hollywood.com

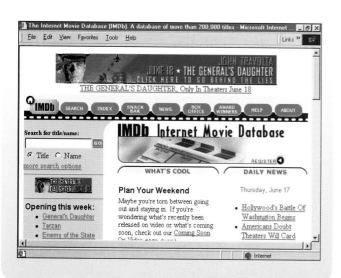

### Internet Movie Database

This database of movie information is sure to have the movie details you want to know.

**URL** us.imdb.com

### MCA/Universal

Find out what's new at this major movie studio.

**URL** www.mca.com

### Movie Clichés List

A large collection of Hollywood clichés.

**URL** www.like.it/vertigo/cliches.html

### Movie Critic

Rate movies you have already seen and find out which movies are worth seeing.

**URL** www.moviecritic.com

### M.O.V.I.E. Trivia/Games

A games gallery and trivia contest where you can win prizes for your film knowledge. You can also buy M.O.V.I.E. merchandise to help support the making of independent movies.

**URL** www.moviefund.com/trivia.html

### Moviefone.com

Find out what's playing at a theater near you.

**URL** www.moviefone.com

### MovieWEB

Previews of upcoming movies, movie merchandise and more.

**URL** www.movieweb.com

### Mr. Showbiz

This site provides excellent information on the latest films.

**URL** mrshowbiz.go.com

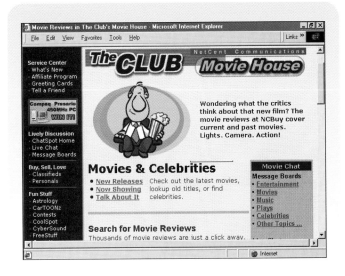

### Paramount Pictures

Contains information on Paramount movies and television.

**URL** www.paramount.com

### Roger Ebert on Movies

Search for this famous reviewer's opinions on films from 1985 to the present or check out the One Minute Movie Reviews of the latest releases.

**URL** www.suntimes.com/ebert

### The Club Movie House

You can find plenty of reviews on both new and old movies at this site!

**URL** www.ncbuy.com/theclub/movies

### Wallywood.com

Wondering what Hollywood is really like? Get a look inside this famous movie mecca and find out where to go or what to do if you ever visit.

**URL** www.wallywood.com

## MUSEUMS

### Andy Warhol Museum

A site dedicated to one of America's most famous artists.

**URL** www.clpgh.org/warhol

### Calvert Marine Museum

Be sure to check out the *highlight* of this gallery: the lighthouses!

**URL** www.calvertmarinemuseum.com

### Computer Museum

This museum includes interactive exhibits, the history of computers and much more.

**URL** www.net.org

### Cookie Museum

Munch your way through this museum! An exclusive showing of experimental cookie art.

**URL** www.chipsahoy.com/cookiemuseum

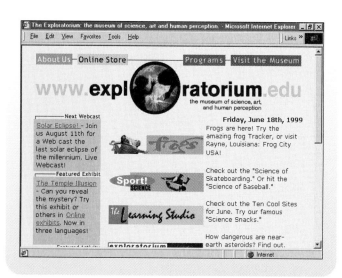

### Exploratorium

A museum of art, science and human perception.

**URL** www.exploratorium.edu

### Franklin Institute Science Museum

This is an interactive museum where you can see many online science exhibits.

**URL** sln.fi.edu

### Global Children's Art Gallery

A spectacular collection of children's artwork!

**URL** www.naturalchild.com/gallery

### Kruger Street Toy & Train Museum

Makes you feel like a kid again. See if you recognize any of these little gems!

**URL** www.toyandtrain.com

## Louvre Museum

A must see! A wonderful collection of some of the world's best art.

**URL** www.louvre.fr

## Metropolitan Museum of Art

This famous New York City museum displays works of art from its impressive collection.

**URL** www.metmuseum.org

## Natural History Museum

Step back in time and mingle with dinosaurs, check out ancient fossils and ponder the evolution of man.

**URL** www.nhm.ac.uk

## Smithsonian Institution

Visit numerous exhibits, critique famous art or monkey around at the National Zoo. There's something for everyone here!

**URL** www.si.edu

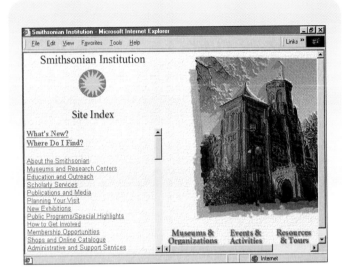

## Tallahassee Antique Car Museum

Remember the 1951 Lincoln Custom Street Rod? How about the Studebaker? Take a ride back in time!

**URL** www.tacm.com

## United States Holocaust Memorial Museum

A museum dedicated to the Holocaust.

**URL** www.ushmm.org

## MUSIC

### CDNOW

You can buy your CDs online at this site.

**URL** www.cdnow.com

### Classical Net

This site includes everything from a composer index to a beginner's guide to collecting classical CDs.

**URL** www.classical.net

### Geffen/DGC Records

Get the latest scoop on bands and see when your favorite band is coming to your town!

**URL** www.geffen.com

### Global Electronic Music Marketplace

Looking for a great deal on a hard-to-find album? Start your search here and compare prices from over 2,000 sellers!

**URL** www.gemm.com

### Guitar.net

This site offers great resources for guitar enthusiasts.

**URL** www.guitar.net

### Internet Underground Music Archive

This site offers information on all types of music, from heavy metal to easy listening.

**URL** www.iuma.com

### Jazz Online

If you're not into rock music, Jazz Online offers a fresh alternative.

**URL** www.jazzonln.com

### L.A. Philharmonic

Symphony music fans will enjoy the Los Angeles Philharmonic's home on the Internet.

**URL** www.laphil.org

### MusicSearch

Whether you're looking for information on Aerosmith or Zappa, start your search here and you'll find what you're looking for!

**URL** www.musicsearch.com

### PolyGram U.S.

Find information on your favorite band and even listen to sound clips.

**URL** www.polygram.com/polygram

### Rock and Roll Hall of Fame

This music museum in Cleveland has an A+ site.

**URL** www.rockhall.com

### Rock Online

Chat with your favorite band, listen to sound clips or purchase CDs at this rocking Web site.

**URL** www.rockonline.com/emi

### Roughstock's History of Country Music

A great presentation of country music history from the 1930s to the present. Be sure to check out the images, sounds and song lyrics.

**URL** www.roughstock.com/history

### Sony Online

Read about Michael Jackson, Mariah Carey, Michael Bolton and lots of other artists.

**URL** www.sony.com

### TicketMaster Online

Find out when your favorite band is coming to town.

**URL** U.S. www.ticketmaster.com
**URL** Canada www.ticketmaster.ca

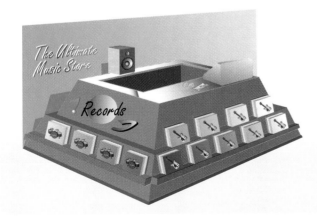

### Warner Bros. Records

Like the Sony site, Warner lets you browse through information on your favorite artists.

**URL** www.wbr.com

# NEWS

### ClariNet Communications Corp.

A popular service that provides the latest news on the Net.

**URL** www.clarinet.com

### CNET: The Computer Network

The online site of CNET, the computer show on cable.

**URL** www.cnet.com

### CNN Interactive

CNN is one of the world's most popular all-news television networks. This site is full of articles, updates and video clips.

**URL** www.cnn.com

### MSNBC

An up-to-the-minute source for news, sports, business and more. Enter your zip code for local news and weather updates.

**URL** www.msnbc.com

### National Public Radio

Check out the schedule of news, talk shows and special features on National Public Radio.

**URL** www.npr.org

### New York Times

An online version of the New York Times.

**URL** nytimes.com

### NewsPage

NewsPage provides you with current, pre-sorted news across a broad array of topics and industries.

**URL** www.newspage.com

### Top 100 Newspapers

This great site provides links to the Top 100 newspapers in the United States.

**URL** www.interest.com/top100.html

### USA Today

This site offers all of the latest news free to the public.

**URL** www.usatoday.com

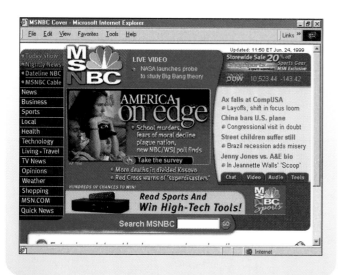

### Yahoo! News

Look here for the latest news, entertainment, sports and much more.

**URL** dailynews.yahoo.com

# RELIGION

### Bible Gateway
Search the Bible in many different languages.
**URL** www.gospelcom.net/bible

### BuddhaNet
This site provides answers to common questions about Buddhism.
**URL** www.buddhanet.net

### Christus Rex et Redemptor Mundi
A collection of Christian information and writings.
**URL** www.christusrex.org

### IslamiCity in Cyberspace
Rich graphics, theological tenets, news articles, chat rooms and more form a support network for the Islamic community.
**URL** www.islamic.org

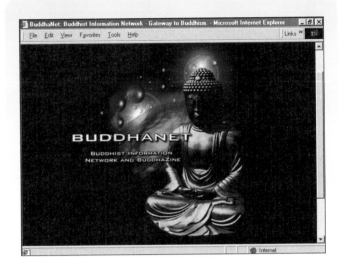

### Jerusalem Mosaic
Take a virtual tour of Jerusalem.
**URL** www1.huji.ac.il/jeru/jerusalem.html

### Jewish.Community
Your Jewish place in cyberspace.
**URL** www.jewish.com

### Monastery of Christ in the Desert
A group of monks in the Santa Fe desert have their own Web site.
**URL** www.christdesert.org

### Scrolls From the Dead Sea
Browse through an exhibit of ancient scrolls.
**URL** sunsite.unc.edu/expo/deadsea.scrolls.exhibit/intro.html

### Secular Web

A source of information for atheists.

**URL** www.infidels.org

### Sikhism Home Page

A guide to a popular Eastern religion.

**URL** www.sikhs.org

# S EARCH TOOLS

### AltaVista

Quickly search millions of Web pages and thousands of newsgroups.

**URL** www.altavista.com

### AOL.COM

This popular Web site is a useful search tool and a whole lot more! Take advantage of AOL's many services while you search for information on the Web.

**URL** www.aol.com

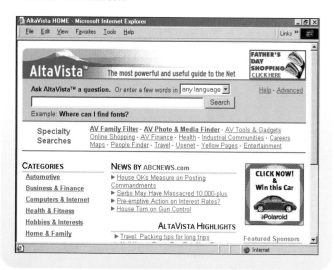

### Deja.com

A tool for searching newsgroup articles.

**URL** www.deja.com

### Dogpile

Use Dogpile to fetch information about the topic of your choice. You won't be barking up the wrong tree with this search tool!

**URL** www.dogpile.com

### GoTo.com

Where searching is simple.

**URL** www.goto.com

### HotBot

Search by keyword or by category at this popular search tool and you'll have loads of information at your fingertips.

**URL** www.hotbot.com

### Magellan Internet Guide

This is a well-indexed guide to the Web.

**URL** magellan.excite.com

### Snap

High-quality search results in a snap! This powerful search tool from NBC Internet enables you to find the information you want with its clearly organized Web directory and keyword searches.

**URL** www.snap.com

### WebCrawler

This could be the Internet search tool for you.

**URL** webcrawler.com

### WhoWhere?

Need to know someone's e-mail address? Check out this useful site.

**URL** www.whowhere.com

### Yack!

Yearn to yak? This specialized search tool enables you to find gab-buddies at live Internet events and chats of your choice.

**URL** www.yack.com

### Yahoo! People Search

Looking for someone on the Internet? Visit this site to access millions of e-mail addresses.

**URL** www.people.yahoo.com

## SEARCH TOOLS: WEB PORTALS

### Excite

Excite lets you search for information that will excite you.

**URL** www.excite.com

### Go Network

A useful site that brings the best of the Internet to one easy-to-use place.

**URL** www.go.com

## Lycos

Not only is this a great place to start your Web search, but you can also read the news, shop, win prizes and more.

**URL** www.lycos.com

## Yahoo!

The ever-popular Internet directory.

**URL** www.yahoo.com

## SPORTS

### DiveNet.com

World Wide Divers' Network.

**URL** divenet.com

### ESPN.com

This site provides all a sports fan could want: scores, pictures, schedules and more.

**URL** www.espn.go.com

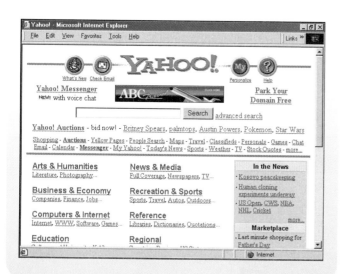

### Fogdog Sports

Buy equipment for sports such as baseball, camping and skiing.

**URL** www.fogdog.com

### Football.com

From high school football to the pros, from fantasy football to the latest news, touch down here for your football fix.

**URL** www.football.com

### GolfWeb

A complete golf information service.

**URL** www.golfweb.com

### GreatOutdoors.com

Get out there! Climbing, cycling, sailing, snowboarding. If you want the dirt on outdoor action and adventure, this site's for you.

**URL** www.greatoutdooors.com

## Major League Baseball Official Site

If you can't get out to the ball game, this is the next best thing. Stats, live audiocasts and all the latest news about the boys of summer.

**URL** www.majorleaguebaseball.com

## NBA

Find information on your favorite teams and players from the NBA.

**URL** www.nba.com

## NBC Sports

NBC brings its quality sports reporting to the Web.

**URL** www.nbc.com/sports

## NHL Official Site

At this site, you will find schedules, contests and the latest news.

**URL** www.nhl.com

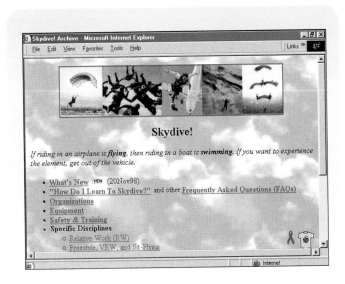

## NHLPA

The National Hockey League Players' Association provides statistics and information on players.

**URL** www.nhlpa.com

## Online Sports

Whether you want to tackle that deal on a unique collector's item or gear up for the upcoming sports season, this is the place to do it. From autographed memorabilia to a new career, you can find it here.

**URL** www.onlinesports.com

## Skydive!

Like bungee jumping, but without the bungee.

**URL** www.afn.org/skydive

## SportsNews.com

This site features what's new in sports today.

**URL** www.sportsnews.com

RS

### Surfing News

The latest news from the surfing world, including tournament standings, global surf links and more.

**URL** holoholo.org/surfnews

### The Sporting News

Every major sport is covered here! Get the most up-to-date information about your favorite events.

**URL** www.sportingnews.com

### USA Today Sports

Find the top sports stories from USA Today.

**URL** www.usatoday.com/sports/sfront.htm

### USGA

The United States Golf Association is a great place to tee-off your search for golf information.

**URL** www.usga.org

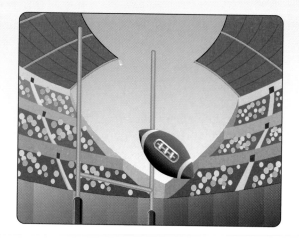

### VeloNews Interactive

A well-designed site covering everything about the world of bicycle racing.

**URL** www.velonews.com

### Volleyball World Wide

Bump, set, spike, surf.

**URL** www.volleyball.org

# TELEVISION

### ABC.com

Visit this site for the latest scoop on ABC television shows! Find episode guides, cast bios, show information and much more!

**URL** abc.go.com

### Academy of Television Arts & Sciences

The official site of the Emmys.

**URL** www.emmys.org

### BBC Online

Find out what the British are watching on TV and listening to on the radio.

**URL** www.bbc.co.uk

### Black Entertainment Television

Television programming focusing on the African-American population.

**URL** www.betnetworks.com

### Cable ThisWeek

Find out what's worth watching at this extensive cable television Web site!

**URL** coyote.accessnv.com/bobf

### CBS.com

Find out what's on the CBS network.

**URL** www.cbs.com

### Columbia Tristar Television

Visit this site for information on shows such as Dawson's Creek, Wheel of Fortune and Days of our Lives!

**URL** www.spe.sony.com/tv

### Comedy Central

The nutty cable channel has its own Web site full of laughs.

**URL** www.comcentral.com

### Commercial Archive

Catch some of the best television commercials of all time at this unique Web site!

**URL** www.commercial-archive.com

### CourtTV Online

All trials, all the time.

**URL** www.courttv.com

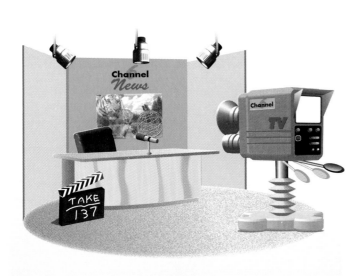

RS

TU

### Discovery Channel

The Canadian and American branches of the Discovery Channel each have their own Web site.

**URL** U.S.     www.discovery.com
**URL** Canada  www.discovery.ca

### FOX.com

This site has information on shows such as The X-Files, Ally McBeal and The Simpsons.

**URL** www.foxnetwork.com

### iQVC Shop

The home-shopping channel. QVC features a large collection of products and some spectacular deals.

**URL** www.qvc.com

### MTV Online

MTV's site provides great graphics and a schedule of programs.

**URL** www.mtv.com

### NBC.com

Find information on popular NBC shows such as Frasier, Friends, ER and more.

**URL** www.nbc.com

### Oprah

The official site for Oprah Winfrey's popular talk show.

**URL** www.oprah.com

### PBS Online

Check out the latest programs, take the trivia challenge and much more at this site.

**URL** www.pbs.org

### SCIFI.COM

This site has information on the Sci-Fi channel and science-fiction in general.

**URL** www.scifi.com

### Showtime No Limits

Find information, reviews and schedules for this large cable network.

**URL** showtimeonline.com

### Simpsons Archive

Homer, Marge, Bart, Lisa and Maggie.

**URL** www.snpp.com

### Star Trek

For an experience that's out of this world, visit this site on the Galaxy Wide Web! Check out your daily briefing and read about everything you've ever wanted to know about Star Trek.

**URL** www.startrek.com

### Today

Includes news articles, recipes from the kitchen and much more from the popular morning show.

**URL** www.msnbc.com/news/TODAY_Front.asp?a

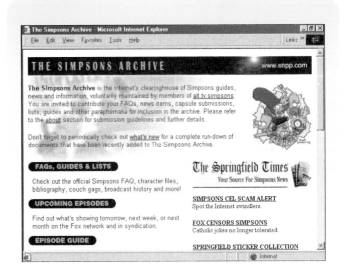

### Tonight Show with Jay Leno

This site is updated every day with the latest jokes and scheduled guests.

**URL** www.nbctonightshow.com

### Travel Channel

Get away from it all. This site offers travel tips and expert advice as well as program information.

**URL** www.travelchannel.com

### TVNow

Primetime picks, celebrity interviews, a movie database and much more!

**URL** www.tv-now.com

### Ultimate TV

If you are looking for a Web site for a particular program, look no further.

**URL** www.ultimatetv.com

### Weather Channel

Weather reports from around the U.S.

**URL** www.weather.com

### X-Files

This popular television show has many sites on the Web with pictures, sound and information.

**URL** www.x-files.com

## THEATER

### Andrew Lloyd Webber

Learn about Sir Andrew himself, read up on his famous musicals like Cats and Phantom of the Opera or hear recordings online.

**URL** www.reallyuseful.com

### Dramatic Exchange

A place to review the works of playwrights.

**URL** www.dramex.org

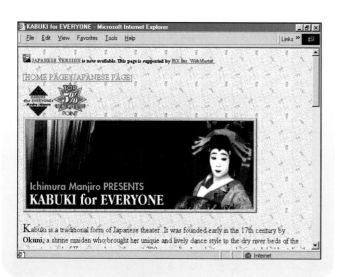

### Gilbert & Sullivan Archive

Find information on musicals like H.M.S. Pinafore.

**URL** diamond.idbsu.edu/gas/GaS.html

### Kabuki for Everyone

Learn more about this traditional Japanese form of theater through the pictures, sounds and movies presented here.

**URL** www.fix.co.jp/kabuki

### Les Misérables

This site has information about the musical based on the famous French novel.

**URL** www.lesmis.com

### Mr. William Shakespeare and the Internet

A good place to start if you want to learn more about Shakespeare.

**URL** www.daphne.palomar.edu/shakespeare

### Musicals.Net

Song lists, links and discussions about your favorite musicals.

**URL** musicals.net

### NH Green Room

Tired of waiting in the Green Room? Take a break and browse through this site! You'll find audition advice, drama workshops and much more.

**URL** www.nhgreenroom.com

### On Broadway Information Page

A list of the shows currently playing in the Big Apple.

**URL** www.on-broadway.com

### Playbill Online

A great source of theater news and information from the company that creates the programs for most Broadway shows.

**URL** www.playbill.com

### Screenwriters & Playwrights

All kinds of resources for all kinds of writers.

**URL** www.teleport.com/~cdeemer/
scrwriter.html

### Thespians.com

Are you a budding actor? Find out about theatrical auditions and productions in your area.

**URL** www.thespians.com

## TRAVEL

### American Airlines

Find flight schedules, information and much more at this site.

**URL** www.aa.com

### Concierge.com

A guide to trips around the world.

**URL** www.concierge.com

**TU**

TRAVEL *continued*

### Geographia

Looking for a travel destination that is off the beaten track? Check out this site for exciting travel ideas.

**URL** www.geographia.com

### History Channel Traveler

Put some history into your next trip! From Civil War landmarks to pop culture sites, this online guide is full of interesting travel destinations.

**URL** www.historytravel.com

### Southwest Airlines

Find information on the cities Southwest flies to, learn their policies and more at this site.

**URL** www.iflyswa.com

### Subway Navigator

How to get from A to B via the subway in over 50 cities around the world.

**URL** www5.wind.ne.jp/n-konno/tube/english.html

### Switzerland

Learn all about this small country located in the center of Western Europe.

**URL** www.yoodle.ch

### Travel Source

A huge travel guide with everything from airlines to scuba diving tours.

**URL** www.travelsource.com

### Travel Warnings & Consular Information Sheets

This site provides travel information for countries around the world. It also lets you know which countries to avoid due to disease, war and natural disasters.

**URL** travel.state.gov/travel_warnings.html

### Web Travel Review

First-hand accounts from people who have traveled to countries around the world.

**URL** www.photo.net/webtravel

# WINDOWS

## Microsoft

The giant company behind Windows.
See what Bill Gates is up to these days!
**URL** www.microsoft.com

## Microsoft Network

Information on The Microsoft Network and
the Internet.
**URL** www.msn.com

## Windows Magazine

An online Windows publication with the
latest computer news, Windows tips and
other neat features.
**URL** www.winmag.com

## Windows Registry Guide

Tips, tricks and troubleshooting advice to
help you get the most out of your Windows
system.
**URL** www.regedit.com

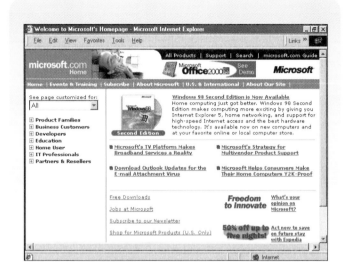

## WinFiles.com

An excellent site with a huge amount of
Windows information, drivers and programs.
**URL** www.winfiles.com

## WinPlanet

A great resource for information on all
versions of Windows, including program
reviews, software news and more.
**URL** www.winplanet.com

## WinSite

A searchable collection of Windows
software for almost anything you could
want, from Web page design programs
to animated screen savers.
**URL** www.winsite.com

## WinZip

The home page of the file compression
program for Windows.
**URL** www.winzip.com

**TU**

**VW**

# INDEX

# INDEX

# INDEX

# INDEX

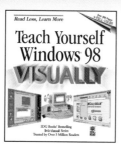

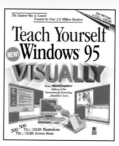
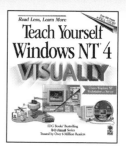

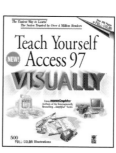

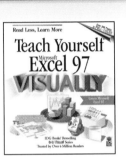
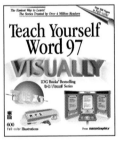

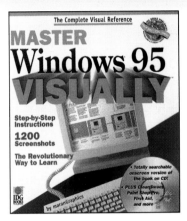

**IDG BOOKS** ®

**TRADE & INDIVIDUAL ORDERS**

Phone: **(800) 762-2974**
or **(317) 596-5200**
*(8 a.m. – 6 p.m., CST, weekdays)*
FAX : **(800) 550-2747**
or **(317) 596-5692**

**EDUCATIONAL ORDERS & DISCOUNTS**

Phone: **(800) 434-2086**
*(8:30 a.m.–5:00 p.m., CST, weekdays)*
FAX : **(317) 596-5499**

**CORPORATE ORDERS FOR 3-D VISUAL™ SERIES**

Phone: **(800) 469-6616**
*(8 a.m.–5 p.m., EST, weekdays)*
FAX : **(905) 890-9434**

| Qty | ISBN | Title | Price | Total |
|-----|------|-------|-------|-------|
|  |  |  |  |  |
|  |  |  |  |  |
|  |  |  |  |  |
|  |  |  |  |  |
|  |  |  |  |  |
|  |  |  |  |  |
|  |  |  |  |  |
|  |  |  |  |  |
|  |  |  |  |  |
|  |  |  |  |  |
|  |  |  |  |  |
|  |  |  |  |  |
|  |  |  |  |  |
|  |  |  |  |  |
|  |  |  |  |  |
|  |  |  |  |  |

### Shipping & Handling Charges

|  | Description | First book | Each add'l. book | Total |
|--|-------------|-----------|------------------|-------|
| *Domestic* | Normal | $4.50 | $1.50 | $ |
|  | Two Day Air | $8.50 | $2.50 | $ |
|  | Overnight | $18.00 | $3.00 | $ |
| *International* | Surface | $8.00 | $8.00 | $ |
|  | Airmail | $16.00 | $16.00 | $ |
|  | DHL Air | $17.00 | $17.00 | $ |

**Subtotal** _____

*CA residents add
applicable sales tax* _____

*IN, MA and MD
residents add
5% sales tax* _____

*IL residents add
6.25% sales tax* _____

*RI residents add
7% sales tax* _____

*TX residents add
8.25% sales tax* _____

*Shipping* _____

**Total** _____

**Ship to:**

Name _____

Address _____

Company _____

City/State/Zip _____

Daytime Phone _____

**Payment:** ☐ Check to IDG Books (US Funds Only)
☐ Visa  ☐ Mastercard  ☐ American Express

Card # _____ Exp. _____ Signature _____

**maranGraphics™**